RACE AGAINST THE MACHINE

How The Digital Revolution Is Accelerating
Innovation, Driving Productivity, and
Irreversibly Transforming Employment and
the Economy

Erik Brynjolfsson and Andrew McAfee

Digital Frontier Press
Lexington, Massachusetts

For information about quantity discounts, email info@raceagainstthemachine.com

www.RaceAgainstTheMachine.com

Library of Congress Cataloging-in-Publication Data

Brynjolfsson, Erik
Race against the machine : how the digital revolution is accelerating innovation, driving productivity, and irreversibly transforming employment and the economy
p. cm.

ISBN 978-0984725113
  1. Technological innovations – Economic Aspects.   I. McAfee, Andrew.
     II. Title.

CONTENTS

To my parents, Ari and Marguerite Brynjolfsson, who always believed in me.

To my father, David McAfee, who showed me that there's nothing better than a job well done.

CHAPTER 1.

TECHNOLOGY'S INFLUENCE ON EMPLOYMENT AND THE ECONOMY

If, in like manner, the shuttle would weave and the plectrum touch the lyre without a hand to guide them, chief workmen would not want servants.

— Aristotle

This is a book about how information technologies are affecting jobs, skills, wages, and the economy. To understand why this is a vital subject, we need only look at the recent statistics about job growth in the United States.

By the late summer of 2011, the U.S. economy had reached a point where even bad news seemed good. The government released a report showing that 117,000 jobs had been created in July. This represented an improvement over May and June, when fewer than 100,000 total jobs had been created, so the report was well received. A headline in the August 6 edition of the *New York Times* declared, "US Reports Solid Job Growth."

Behind those rosy headlines, however, lay a thorny problem. The 117,000 new jobs weren't even enough to keep up with population growth, let alone reemploy any of the approximately 12 million Americans who had lost their jobs in the Great Recession of 2007-2009. Economist Laura D'Andrea Tyson calculated that even if job creation almost doubled, to the 208,000 jobs per month experienced throughout 2005, it would take until 2023 to close the gap opened by the recession. Job creation at the level observed during July of 2011, on the other hand, would ensure only an ever-smaller percentage of employed Americans over time. And in September the government reported that absolutely no net new jobs had been created in August.

Of all the grim statistics and stories accompanying the Great Recession and subsequent recovery, those related to employment were the worst. Recessions always increase joblessness, of course, but between May 2007 and October 2009 unemployment jumped by more than 5.7 percentage points, the largest increase in the postwar period.

An Economy That's Not Putting People Back to Work

An even bigger problem, however, was that the unemployed couldn't find work even after economic growth resumed. In July of 2011, 25 months after the recession officially ended, the main U.S. unemployment rate remained at 9.1%, less than 1 percentage point better than it was at its worst point. The mean length of time unemployed had skyrocketed to 39.9 weeks by the middle of 2011, a duration almost twice as long as that observed during any previous postwar recovery. And the workforce participation rate, or proportion of working-age adults with jobs, fell below 64%—a level not seen since 1983 when women had not yet entered the labor force in large numbers.

Everyone agreed that this was a dire problem. Nobel Prize-winning economist Paul Krugman described unemployment as a "terrible scourge ... a continuing tragedy. ... How can we expect to prosper two decades from now when millions of young graduates are, in effect, being denied the chance to get started on their careers?"

Writing in *The Atlantic*, Don Peck described chronic unemployment as "a pestilence that slowly eats away at people, families, and, if it spreads widely enough, the fabric of society. Indeed, history suggests that it is perhaps society's most noxious ill. ... This era of high joblessness ... is likely to warp our politics, our culture, and the character of our society for many years." His colleague Megan McArdle asked her readers to visualize people who had been unemployed for a long time: "Think about what is happening to millions of people out there ... whose savings and social networks are exhausted (or were never very big to begin with), who are in their fifties and not old enough to retire, but very hard to place with an employer who will pay them as much as they were worth to their old firm. Think of the people who can't support their children, or themselves. Think of their despair."

Many Americans did think of such people. Twenty-four percent of respondents to a June 2011 Gallup poll identified "unemployment/jobs" as the most important problem facing America (this in addition to the 36% identifying "economy in general").

The grim unemployment statistics puzzled many because other measures of business health rebounded pretty quickly after the Great Recession officially ended in June 2009. GDP growth averaged 2.6% in the seven quarters after the recession's end, a rate 75% as high as the long-term average over 1948-2007. U.S. corporate profits reached new records. And by 2010, investment in equipment and software returned to 95% of its historical peak, the fastest recovery of equipment investment in a generation.

Economic history teaches that when companies grow, earn profits, and buy equipment, they also typically hire workers. But American companies didn't resume hiring after the Great Recession ended. The volume of layoffs quickly returned to pre-recession levels, so companies stopped shedding workers. But the number of new hires remained severely depressed. Companies brought new machines in, but not new people.

Where Did the Jobs Go?

Why has the scourge of unemployment been so persistent? Analysts offer three alternative explanations: cyclicality, stagnation, and the "end of work."

The cyclical explanation holds that there's nothing new or mysterious going on; unemployment in America remains so high simply because the economy is not growing quickly enough to put people back to work. Paul Krugman is one of the prime advocates of this explanation. As he writes, "All the facts suggest that high unemployment in America is the result of inadequate demand— full stop." Former Office of Management and Budget director Peter Orszag agrees, writing that "the fundamental impediment to getting jobless Americans back to work is weak growth." In the cyclical explanation, an especially deep drop in demand like the Great Recession is bound to be followed by a long and frustratingly slow recovery. What America has been experiencing since 2007, in short, is another case of the business cycle in action, albeit a particularly painful one.

A second explanation for current hard times sees stagnation, not cyclicality, in action. Stagnation in this context means a long-term decline in America's ability to innovate and increase productivity. Economist Tyler Cowen articulates this view in his 2010 book, *The Great Stagnation:*

> We are failing to understand why we are failing. All of these problems have a single, little noticed root cause: We have been living off low-hanging fruit for at least three hundred years. ... Yet during the last forty years, that low-hanging fruit started disappearing, and we started pretending it was still there. We have failed to recognize that we are at a technological plateau and the trees are more bare than we would like to think. That's it. That is what has gone wrong.

To support his view, Cowen cites the declining median income of American families. Median income is a halfway point; there are as many families making less than this amount as there are making more. The growth of median income slowed down significantly at least 30 years ago, and actually declined during the first decade of this century; the average family in America earned less in 2009 than it did in 1999. Cowen attributes this slowdown to the fact that the economy has reached a "technological plateau."

Writing in the *Harvard Business Review,* Leo Tilman and the Nobel Prize-winning economist Edmund Phelps agreed with this stagnation: "[America's] dynamism—its ability and proclivity to innovate—has brought economic inclusion by creating numerous jobs. It has also brought real prosperity—engaging, challenging jobs and careers of self-realization and self-discovery ... [but] dynamism has been in decline over the past decade."

The stagnation argument doesn't ignore the Great Recession, but also doesn't believe that it's the principle cause of the current slow recovery and high joblessness. These woes have a more fundamental source: a slowdown in the kinds of powerful new ideas that drive economic progress.

This slowdown pre-dates the Great Recession. In *The Great Stagnation*, in fact, Cowen maintained that it's been going on since the 1970s, when U.S. productivity growth slowed and the median income of American families stopped rising as quickly as it had in the past. Cowen, Phelps, and other "stagnationists" hold that only higher rates of innovation and technical progress will lift the economy out of its current doldrums.

A variant on this explanation is not that America has stagnated, but that other nations such as India and China have begun to catch up. In a global economy, America businesses and workers can't earn a premium if they don't have greater productivity than their counterparts in other nations. Technology has eliminated many of the barriers of geography and ignorance that previously kept capitalists and consumers from finding the lowest price inputs and products anywhere in the world. The result has been a great equalization in factor prices like wages, raising salaries in developing nations and forcing American labor to compete on different terms. Nobel prize winner Michael Spence has analyzed this phenomenon and its implications for convergence in living standards.

The third explanation for America's current job creation problems flips the stagnation argument on its head, seeing not too little recent technological progress, but instead too much. We'll call this the "end of work" argument, after Jeremy Rifkin's 1995 book of the same title. In it, Rifkin laid out a bold and disturbing hypothesis: that "we are entering a new phase in world history— one in which fewer and fewer workers will be needed to produce the goods and services for the global population."

Computers caused this important shift. "In the years ahead," Rifkin wrote, "more sophisticated software technologies are going to bring civilization ever closer to a near-workerless world. ... Today, all ... sectors of the economy ... are experiencing technological displacement, forcing millions onto the unemployment rolls." Coping with this displacement, he wrote, was "likely to be the single most pressing social issue of the coming century."

The end-of-work argument has been made by, among many others, economist John Maynard Keynes, management theorist Peter Drucker, and Nobel Prize winner Wassily Leontief, who stated in 1983 that "the role of humans as the most important factor of production is bound to diminish in the same way that the role of horses in agricultural production was first diminished and then eliminated by the introduction of tractors." In his 2009 book *The Lights in the Tunnel,* software executive Martin Ford agreed, stating that "at some point in the future—it might be many years or decades from now—machines will be able to do the jobs of a large percentage of the 'average' people in our population, and these people will not be able to find new jobs." Brian Arthur argues that a vast, but largely invisible "second economy" already exists in the form of digital automation.

The end-of-work argument is an intuitively appealing one; every time we get cash from an ATM instead of a teller or use an automated kiosk to check in at an airport for a flight, we see evidence that technology displaces human labor. But low unemployment levels in the United States throughout the 1980s, '90s, and first seven years of the new millennium did much to discredit fears of displacement, and it has not been featured in the mainstream discussion of today's jobless recovery. For example, a 2010 report published by the Federal Reserve Bank of Richmond, titled "The Rise in Long-Term Unemployment: Potential Causes and Implications," does not contain the words *computer, hardware, software,* or *technology* in its text. Working papers published in 2011 by the International Monetary Fund, titled "New Evidence on Cyclical and Structural Sources of Unemployment" and "Has the Great Recession Raised U.S. Structural Unemployment?" are similarly silent about technology. As technology journalist Farhad Manjoo summarized in the online magazine *Slate,* "Most economists aren't taking these worries very seriously. The idea that computers might significantly disrupt human labor markets—and, thus, further weaken the global economy—so far remains on the fringes."

Our Goal: Bringing Technology into the Discussion

We think it's time to bring this idea into the mainstream and to pay more attention to technology's impact on skills, wages, and employment. We certainly agree that a Great Recession implies a long recovery, and that current sluggish demand is in large part to blame for today's lack of jobs. But cyclical weak demand is not the whole story. The stagnationists are right that longer and deeper trends are also at work. The Great Recession has made them more visible, but they've been going on for a while.

The stagnationists correctly point out that median income and other important measures of American economic health stopped growing robustly some time ago, but we disagree with them about why this has happened. They think it's because the pace of technological innovation has slowed down. We think it's because the pace has sped up so much that it's left a lot of people behind. Many workers, in short, are losing the race against the machine.

And it's not just workers. Technological progress—in particular, improvements in computer hardware, software, and networks—has been so rapid and so surprising that many present-day organizations, institutions, policies, and mindsets are not keeping up. Viewed through this lens, the increase in globalization is not an alternative explanation, but rather one of the consequences of the increased power and ubiquity of technology.

So we agree with the end-of-work crowd that computerization is bringing deep changes, but we're not as pessimistic as they are. We don't believe in the coming obsolescence of all human workers. In fact, some human skills are more valuable than ever, even in an age of incredibly powerful and capable digital technologies. But other skills have become worthless, and people who hold the wrong ones now find that they have little to offer employers. They're losing the race against the machine, a fact reflected in today's employment statistics.

We wrote this book because we believe that digital technologies are one of the most important driving forces in the economy today. They're transforming the world of work and are key drivers of productivity and growth. Yet their impact on employment is not well understood, and definitely not fully appreciated. When people talk about jobs in America today, they talk about cyclicality, outsourcing and off-shoring, taxes and regulation, and the wisdom and efficacy of different kinds of stimulus. We don't doubt the importance of all these factors. The economy is a complex, multifaceted entity.

But there has been relatively little talk about role of acceleration of technology. It may seem paradoxical that faster progress can hurt wages and jobs for millions of people, but we argue that's what's been happening. As we'll show, computers are now doing many things that used to be the domain of people only. The pace and scale of this encroachment into human skills is relatively recent and has profound economic implications. Perhaps the most important of these is that while digital progress grows the overall economic pie, it can do so while leaving some people, or even a lot of them, worse off.

And computers (hardware, software, and networks) are only going to get more powerful and capable in the future, and have an ever-bigger impact on jobs, skills, and the economy. The root of our problems is not that we're in a Great Recession, or a Great Stagnation, but rather that we are in the early throes of a Great Restructuring. Our technologies are racing ahead but many of our skills and organizations are lagging behind. So it's urgent that we understand these phenomena, discuss their implications, and come up with strategies that allow human workers to race ahead with machines instead of racing against them.

Here's how we'll proceed through the rest of this book:

Humanity and Technology on the Second Half of the Chessboard

Why are computers racing ahead of workers now? And what, if anything, can be done about it? Chapter 2 discusses digital technology, giving examples of just how astonishing recent developments have been and showing how they have upset well-established ideas about what computers are and aren't good at.

What's more, the progress we've experienced augurs even larger advances in coming years. We explain the sources of this progress, and also its limitations.

Creative Destruction: The Economics of Accelerating Technology and Disappearing Jobs

Chapter 3 explores the economic implications of these rapid technological advances and the growing mismatches that create both economic winners and losers. It concentrates on three theories that explain how such progress can leave some people behind, even as it benefits society as a whole. There are divergences between higher-skilled and lower-skilled workers, between superstars and everyone else, and between capital and labor. We present evidence that all three divergences are taking place.

What Is to Be Done? Prescriptions and Recommendations

Once technical trends and economic principles are clear, Chapter 4 considers what we can and should do to meet the challenges of high unemployment and other negative consequences of our current race against the machine. We can't win that race, especially as computers continue to become more powerful and capable. But we can learn to better race *with* machines, using them as allies rather than adversaries. We discuss ways to put this principle into practice, concentrating on ways to accelerate organizational innovation and enhance human capital.

Conclusion: The Digital Frontier

We conclude in Chapter 5 on an upbeat note. This might seem odd in a book about jobs and the economy written during a time of high unemployment, stagnant wages, and anemic GDP growth. But this is fundamentally a book about digital technology, and when we look at the full impact of computers and networks, now and in the future, we are very optimistic indeed. These tools are greatly improving our world and our lives, and will continue to do so. We are strong digital optimists, and we want to convince you to be one, too.

CHAPTER 2.
HUMANITY AND TECHNOLOGY
ON THE
SECOND HALF OF THE
CHESSBOARD

Any sufficiently advanced technology is indistinguishable from magic.
— Arthur C. Clarke, 1962

We used to be pretty confident that we knew the relative strengths and weaknesses of computers vis-à-vis humans. But computers have started making inroads in some unexpected areas. This fact helps us to better understand the past few turbulent years and the true impact of digital technologies on jobs.

A good illustration of how much recent technology advances have taken us by surprise comes from comparing a carefully researched book published in 2004 with an announcement made in 2010. The book is *The New Division of Labor* by economists Frank Levy and Richard Murnane. As its title implies, it's a description of the comparative capabilities of computers and human workers.

In the book's second chapter, "Why People Still Matter," the authors present a spectrum of information-processing tasks. At one end are straightforward applications of existing rules. These tasks, such as performing arithmetic, can be easily automated. After all, computers are good at following rules.

At the other end of the complexity spectrum are pattern-recognition tasks where the rules can't be inferred. *The New Division of Labor* gives driving in traffic as an example of this type of task, and asserts that it is not automatable:

> The ... truck driver is processing a constant stream of [visual, aural, and tactile] information from his environment. ... To program this behavior we could begin with a video camera and other sensors to capture the sensory input. But executing a left turn against oncoming traffic involves so many factors that it is hard to imagine discovering the set of rules that can replicate a driver's behavior. ...
>
> Articulating [human] knowledge and embedding it in software for all but highly structured situations are at present enormously difficult tasks. ... Computers cannot easily substitute for humans in [jobs like truck driving].

The results of the first DARPA Grand Challenge, held in 2004, supported Levy and Murnane's conclusion. The challenge was to build a driverless vehicle that could navigate a 150-mile route through the unpopulated Mohave Desert. The "winning" vehicle couldn't even make it eight miles into the course and took hours to go even that far.

In Domain After Domain, Computers Race Ahead

Just six years later, however, real-world driving went from being an example of a task that couldn't be automated to an example of one that had. In October of 2010, Google announced on its official blog that it had modified a fleet of Toyota Priuses to the point that they were fully autonomous cars, ones that had driven more than 1,000 miles on American roads without any human involvement at all, and more than 140,000 miles with only minor inputs from the person behind the wheel. (To comply with driving laws, Google felt that it had to have a person sitting behind the steering wheel at all times).

Levy and Murnane were correct that automatic driving on populated roads *is* an enormously difficult task, and it's *not* easy to build a computer that can substitute for human perception and pattern matching in this domain. Not easy, but not impossible either—this challenge has largely been met.

The Google technologists succeeded not by taking any shortcuts around the challenges listed by Levy and Murnane, but instead by meeting them head-on. They used the staggering amounts of data collected for Google Maps and Google Street View to provide as much information as possible about the roads their cars were traveling. Their vehicles also collected huge volumes of real-time data using video, radar, and LIDAR (light detection and ranging) gear mounted on the car; these data were fed into software that takes into account the rules of the road, the presence, trajectory, and likely identity of all objects in the vicinity, driving conditions, and so on. This software controls the car and probably provides better awareness, vigilance, and reaction times than any human driver could. The Google vehicles' only accident came when the driverless car was rear-ended by a car driven by a human driver as it stopped at a traffic light.

None of this is easy. But in a world of plentiful accurate data, powerful sensors, and massive storage capacity and processing power, it *is* possible. This is the world we live in now. It's one where computers improve so quickly that their capabilities pass from the realm of science fiction into the everyday world not over the course of a human lifetime, or even within the span of a professional's career, but instead in just a few years.

Levy and Murnane give *complex communication* as another example of a human capability that's very hard for machines to emulate. Complex communication entails conversing with a human being, especially in situations that are complicated, emotional, or ambiguous. Evolution has "programmed" people to do this effortlessly, but it's been very hard to program computers to do the same. Translating from one human language to another, for example, has long been a goal of computer science researchers, but progress has been slow because grammar and vocabulary are so complicated and ambiguous.

In January of 2011, however, the translation services company Lionbridge announced pilot corporate customers for GeoFluent, a technology developed in partnership with IBM. GeoFluent takes words written in one language, such as an online chat message from a customer seeking help with a problem, and translates them accurately and immediately into another language, such as the one spoken by a customer service representative in a different country.

GeoFluent is based on statistical machine translation software developed at IBM's Thomas J. Watson Research Center. This software is improved by Lionbridge's digital libraries of previous translations. This "translation memory" makes GeoFluent more accurate, particularly for the kinds of conversations large high-tech companies are likely to have with customers and other parties. One such company tested the quality of GeoFluent's automatic translations of online chat messages. These messages, which concerned the company's products and services, were sent by Chinese and Spanish customers to English-speaking employees. GeoFluent instantly translated them, presenting them in the native language of the receiver. After the chat session ended, both customers and employees were asked whether the automatically translated messages were useful—whether they were clear enough to allow the people to take meaningful action. Approximately 90% reported that they were. In this case, automatic translation was good enough for business purposes.

The Google driverless car shows how far and how fast digital pattern recognition abilities have advanced recently. Lionbridge's

GeoFluent shows how much progress has been made in computers' ability to engage in complex communication. Another technology developed at IBM's Watson labs, this one actually named Watson, shows how powerful it can be to combine these two abilities and how far the computers have advanced recently into territory thought to be uniquely human.

Watson is a supercomputer designed to play the popular game show Jeopardy! in which contestants are asked questions on a wide variety of topics that are not known in advance.[1] In many cases, these questions involve puns and other types of wordplay. It can be difficult to figure out precisely what is being asked, or how an answer should be constructed. Playing Jeopardy! well, in short, requires the ability to engage in complex communication.

The way Watson plays the game also requires massive amounts of pattern matching. The supercomputer has been loaded with hundreds of millions of unconnected digital documents, including encyclopedias and other reference works, newspaper stories, and the Bible. When it receives a question, it immediately goes to work to figure out what is being asked (using algorithms that specialize in complex communication), then starts querying all these documents to find and match patterns in search of the answer. Watson works with astonishing thoroughness and speed, as IBM research manager Eric Brown explained in an interview:

> We start with a single clue, we analyze the clue, and then we go through a candidate generation phase, which actually runs several different primary searches, which each produce on the order of 50 search results. Then, each search result can produce several candidate answers, and so by the time we've generated all of our candidate answers, we might have three to five hundred candidate answers for the clue.

---

[1] To be precise, Jeopardy! contestants are shown answers and must ask questions that would yield these answers.

Now, all of these candidate answers can be processed independently and in parallel, so now they fan out to answer-scoring analytics [that] score the answers. Then, we run additional searches for the answers to gather more evidence, and then run deep analytics on each piece of evidence, so each candidate answer might go and generate 20 pieces of evidence to support that answer.

Now, all of this evidence can be analyzed independently and in parallel, so that fans out again. Now you have evidence being deeply analyzed ... and then all of these analytics produce scores that ultimately get merged together, using a machine-learning framework to weight the scores and produce a final ranked order for the candidate answers, as well as a final confidence in them. Then, that's what comes out in the end.

What comes out in the end is so fast and accurate that even the best human Jeopardy! players simply can't keep up. In February of 2011, Watson played in a televised tournament against the two most accomplished human contestants in the show's history. After two rounds of the game shown over three days, the computer finished with more than three times as much money as its closest flesh-and-blood competitor. One of these competitors, Ken Jennings, acknowledged that digital technologies had taken over the game of Jeopardy! Underneath his written response to the tournament's last question, he added, "I for one welcome our new computer overlords."

Moore's Law and the Second Half of the Chessboard

Where did these overlords come from? How has science fiction become business reality so quickly? Two concepts are essential for understanding this remarkable progress. The first, and better known, is Moore's Law, which is an expansion of an observation made by Gordon Moore, co-founder of microprocessor maker

Intel. In a 1965 article in *Electronics Magazine*, Moore noted that the number of transistors in a minimum-cost integrated circuit had been doubling every 12 months, and predicted that this same rate of improvement would continue into the future. When this proved to be the case, Moore's Law was born.

Later modifications changed the time required for the doubling to occur; the most widely accepted period at present is 18 months. Variations of Moore's Law have been applied to improvement over time in disk drive capacity, display resolution, and network bandwidth. In these and many other cases of digital improvement, doubling happens both quickly and reliably.

It also seems that software progresses at least as fast as hardware does, at least in some domains. Computer scientist Martin Grötschel analyzed the speed with which a standard optimization problem could be solved by computers over the period 1988-2003. He documented a 43 millionfold improvement, which he broke down into two factors: faster processors and better algorithms embedded in software. Processor speeds improved by a factor of 1,000, but these gains were dwarfed by the algorithms, which got 43,000 times better over the same period.

The second concept relevant for understanding recent computing advances is closely related to Moore's Law. It comes from an ancient story about math made relevant to the present age by the innovator and futurist Ray Kurzweil. In one version of the story, the inventor of the game of chess shows his creation to his country's ruler. The emperor is so delighted by the game that he allows the inventor to name his own reward. The clever man asks for a quantity of rice to be determined as follows: one grain of rice is placed on the first square of the chessboard, two grains on the second, four on the third, and so on, with each square receiving twice as many grains as the previous.

The emperor agrees, thinking that this reward was too small. He eventually sees, however, that the constant doubling results in tremendously large numbers. The inventor winds up with $2^{64}-1$ grains of rice, or a pile bigger than Mount Everest. In some versions of the story the emperor is so displeased at being outsmarted that he beheads the inventor.

In his 2000 book *The Age of Spiritual Machines: When Computers Exceed Human Intelligence,* Kurzweil notes that the pile of rice is not that exceptional on the first half of the chessboard:

> After thirty-two squares, the emperor had given the inventor about 4 billion grains of rice. That's a reasonable quantity— about one large field's worth—and the emperor did start to take notice.

> But the emperor could still remain an emperor. And the inventor could still retain his head. It was as they headed into the second half of the chessboard that at least one of them got into trouble.

Kurzweil's point is that constant doubling, reflecting exponential growth, is deceptive because it is initially unremarkable. Exponential increases initially look a lot like standard linear ones, but they're not. As time goes by—as we move into the second half of the chessboard—exponential growth confounds our intuition and expectations. It accelerates far past linear growth, yielding Everest-sized piles of rice and computers that can accomplish previously impossible tasks.

So where are we in the history of business use of computers? Are we in the second half of the chessboard yet? This is an impossible question to answer precisely, of course, but a reasonable estimate yields an intriguing conclusion. The U.S. Bureau of Economic Analysis added "Information Technology" as a category of business investment in 1958, so let's use that as our starting year. And let's take the standard 18 months as the Moore's Law doubling period. Thirty-two doublings then take us to 2006 and to the second half of the chessboard. Advances like the Google autonomous car, Watson the Jeopardy! champion supercomputer, and high-quality instantaneous machine translation, then, can be seen as the first examples of the kinds of digital innovations we'll see as we move further into the second half—into the phase where exponential growth yields jaw-dropping results.

Computing the Economy: The Economic Power of General Purpose Technologies

These results will be felt across virtually every task, job, and industry. Such versatility is a key feature of *general purpose technologies* (GPTs), a term economists assign to a small group of technological innovations so powerful that they interrupt and accelerate the normal march of economic progress. Steam power, electricity, and the internal combustion engine are examples of previous GPTs.

It is difficult to overstate their importance. As the economists Timothy Bresnahan and Manuel Trajtenberg note:

> Whole eras of technical progress and economic growth appear to be driven by ... GPTs, [which are] characterized by pervasiveness (they are used as inputs by many downstream sectors), inherent potential for technical improvements, and "innovational complementarities," meaning that the productivity of R&D in downstream sectors increases as a consequence of innovation in the GPT. Thus, as GPTs improve they spread throughout the economy, bringing about generalized productivity gains.

GPTs, then, not only get better themselves over time (and as Moore's Law shows, this is certainly true of computers), they also lead to complementary innovations in the processes, companies, and industries that make use of them. They lead, in short, to a cascade of benefits that is both broad and deep.

Computers are the GPT of our era, especially when combined with networks and labeled "information and communications technology" (ICT). Economists Susanto Basu and John Fernald highlight how this GPT allows departures from business as usual.

> The availability of cheap ICT capital allows firms to deploy their other inputs in radically different and productivity-enhancing ways. In so doing, cheap computers and telecommunications equipment can foster an ever-expanding sequence of complementary inventions in industries using ICT.

Note that GPTs don't just benefit their "home" industries. Computers, for example, increase productivity not only in the high-tech sector but also in all industries that purchase and use digital gear. And these days, that means essentially all industries; even the least IT-intensive American sectors like agriculture and mining are now spending billions of dollars each year to digitize themselves.

Note also the choice of words by Basu and Fernald: computers and networks bring an *ever-expanding* set of opportunities to companies. Digitization, in other words, is not a single project providing one-time benefits. Instead, it's an ongoing process of creative destruction; innovators use both new and established technologies to make deep changes at the level of the task, the job, the process, even the organization itself. And these changes build and feed on each other so that the possibilities offered really are constantly expanding.

This has been the case for as long as businesses have been using computers, even when we were still in the front half of the chessboard. The personal computer, for example, democratized computing in the early 1980s, putting processing power in the hands of more and more knowledge workers. In the mid-1990s two major innovations appeared: the World Wide Web and large-scale commercial business software like enterprise resource planning (ERP) and customer relationship management (CRM) systems. The former gave companies the ability to tap new markets and sales channels, and also made available more of the world's knowledge than had ever before been possible; the latter let firms redesign their processes, monitor and control far-flung operations, and gather and analyze vast amounts of data.

These advances don't expire or fade away over time. Instead, they get combined with and incorporated into both earlier and later ones, and benefits keep mounting. The World Wide Web, for example, became much more useful to people once Google made it easier to search, while a new wave of social, local, and mobile applications are just emerging. CRM systems have been extended to smart phones so that salespeople can stay connected from the road, and tablet computers now provide much of the functionality of PCs.

The innovations we're starting to see in the second half of the chessboard will also be folded into this ongoing work of business invention. In fact, they already are. The GeoFluent offering from Lionbridge has brought instantaneous machine translation to customer service interactions. IBM is working with Columbia University Medical Center and the University of Maryland School of Medicine to adapt Watson to the work of medical diagnosis, announcing a partnership in that area with voice recognition software maker Nuance. And the Nevada state legislature directed its Department of Motor Vehicles to come up with regulations covering autonomous vehicles on the state's roads. Of course, these are only a small sample of the myriad IT-enabled innovations that are transforming manufacturing, distribution, retailing, media, finance, law, medicine, research, management, marketing, and almost every other economic sector and business function.

Where People Still Win (at Least for Now)

Although computers are encroaching into territory that used to be occupied by people alone, like advanced pattern recognition and complex communication, for now humans still hold the high ground in each of these areas. Experienced doctors, for example, make diagnoses by comparing the body of medical knowledge they've accumulated against patients' lab results and descriptions of symptoms, and also by employing the advanced subconscious pattern recognition abilities we label "intuition." (*Does this patient seem like they're holding something back? Do they look healthy, or is something off about their skin tone or energy level?*) Similarly, the best therapists, managers, and salespeople excel at interacting and communicating with others, and their strategies for gathering information and influencing behavior can be amazingly complex.

But it's also true, as the examples in this chapter show, that as we move deeper into the second half of the chessboard, computers are rapidly getting better at both of these skills. We're starting to see evidence that this digital progress is affecting the business world. A March 2011 story by John Markoff in the *New York Times* highlighted how heavily computers' pattern recognition abilities are already being exploited by the legal industry where, according to one estimate, moving from human to digital labor during the discovery process could let one lawyer do the work of 500.

> In January, for example, Blackstone Discovery of Palo Alto, Calif., helped analyze 1.5 million documents for less than $100,000. ...
>
> "From a legal staffing viewpoint, it means that a lot of people who used to be allocated to conduct document review are no longer able to be billed out," said Bill Herr, who as a lawyer at a major chemical company used to muster auditoriums of lawyers to read documents for weeks on end. "People get bored, people get headaches. Computers don't."

23

> The computers seem to be good at their new jobs. ... Herr ... used e-discovery software to reanalyze work his company's lawyers did in the 1980s and '90s. His human colleagues had been only 60 percent accurate, he found.
>
> "Think about how much money had been spent to be slightly better than a coin toss," he said.

And an article the same month in the *Los Angeles Times* by Alena Semuels highlighted that despite the fact that closing a sale often requires complex communication, the retail industry has been automating rapidly.

> In an industry that employs nearly 1 in 10 Americans and has long been a reliable job generator, companies increasingly are looking to peddle more products with fewer employees. ... Virtual assistants are taking the place of customer service representatives. Kiosks and self-service machines are reducing the need for checkout clerks.
>
> Vending machines now sell iPods, bathing suits, gold coins, sunglasses and razors; some will even dispense prescription drugs and medical marijuana to consumers willing to submit to a fingerprint scan. And shoppers are finding information on touch screen kiosks, rather than talking to attendants. ...
>
> The [machines] cost a fraction of brick-and-mortar stores. They also reflect changing consumer buying habits. Online shopping has made Americans comfortable with the idea of buying all manner of products without the help of a salesman or clerk.

During the Great Recession, nearly 1 in 12 people working in sales in America lost their job, accelerating a trend that had begun long before. In 1995, for example, 2.08 people were employed in "sales and related" occupations for every $1 million of real GDP generated that year. By 2002 (the last year for which consistent data are available), that number had fallen to 1.79, a decline of nearly 14 percent.

If, as these examples indicate, both pattern recognition and complex communication are now so amenable to automation, are *any* human skills immune? Do people have any sustainable comparative advantage as we head ever deeper into the second half of the chessboard? In the physical domain, it seems that we do for the time being. Humanoid robots are still quite primitive, with poor fine motor skills and a habit of falling down stairs. So it doesn't appear that gardeners and restaurant busboys are in danger of being replaced by machines any time soon.

And many physical jobs also require advanced mental abilities; plumbers and nurses engage in a great deal of pattern recognition and problem solving throughout the day, and nurses also do a lot of complex communication with colleagues and patients. The difficulty of automating their work reminds us of a quote attributed to a 1965 NASA report advocating manned space flight: "Man is the lowest-cost, 150-pound, nonlinear, all-purpose computer system which can be mass-produced by unskilled labor."

Even in the domain of pure knowledge work—jobs that don't have a physical component—there's a lot of important territory that computers haven't yet started to cover. In his 2005 book *The Singularity Is Near: When Humans Transcend Biology*, Ray Kurzweil predicts that future computers will "encompass ... the pattern-recognition powers, problem-solving skills, and emotional and moral intelligence of the human brain itself," but so far only the first of these abilities has been demonstrated. Computers so far have proved to be great pattern recognizers but lousy general problem solvers; IBM's supercomputers, for example, couldn't take what they'd learned about chess and apply it to Jeopardy! or any other challenge until they were redesigned, reprogrammed, and fed different data by their human creators.

And for all their power and speed, today's digital machines have shown little creative ability. They can't compose very good songs, write great novels, or generate good ideas for new businesses. Apparent exceptions here only prove the rule. A prankster used an online generator of abstracts for computer science papers to create a submission that was accepted for a technical conference (in fact, the organizers invited the "author" to chair a panel), but the abstract was simply a series of somewhat-related technical terms strung together with a few standard verbal connectors.

Similarly, software that automatically generates summaries of baseball games works well, but this is because much sports writing is highly formulaic and thus amenable to pattern matching and simpler communication. Here's a sample from a program called StatsMonkey:

UNIVERSITY PARK — An outstanding effort by Willie Argo carried the Illini to an 11-5 victory over the Nittany Lions on Saturday at Medlar Field.

Argo blasted two home runs for Illinois. He went 3-4 in the game with five RBIs and two runs scored.

Illini starter Will Strack struggled, allowing five runs in six innings, but the bullpen allowed only no runs and the offense banged out 17 hits to pick up the slack and secure the victory for the Illini.

The difference between the automatic generation of formulaic prose and genuine insight is still significant, as the history of a 60-year-old test makes clear. The mathematician and computer science pioneer Alan Turing considered the question of whether machines could think "too meaningless to deserve discussion," but in 1950 he proposed a test to determine how humanlike a machine could become. The "Turing test" involves a test group of people having online chats with two entities, a human and a computer. If the members of the test group can't in general tell which entity is the machine, then the machine passes the test.

Turing himself predicted that by 2000 computers would be indistinguishable from people 70% of the time in his test. However, at the Loebner Prize, an annual Turing test competition held since 1990, the $25,000 prize for a chat program that can persuade half the judges of its humanity has yet to be awarded. Whatever else computers may be at present, they are not yet convincingly human.

But as the examples in this chapter make clear, computers are now demonstrating skills and abilities that used to belong exclusively to human workers. This trend will only accelerate as we move deeper into the second half of the chessboard. What are the economic implications of this phenomenon? We'll turn our attention to this topic in the next chapter.

Chapter 3.
Creative Destruction:
The Economics of
Accelerating Technology
and Disappearing Jobs

We are being afflicted with a new disease of which some readers may not yet have heard the name, but of which they will hear a great deal in the years to come—namely, technological unemployment. This means unemployment due to our discovery of means of economising the use of labour outrunning the pace at which we can find new uses for labour.

— John Maynard Keynes, 1930

The individual technologies and the broader technological acceleration discussed in Chapter 2 are creating enormous value. There is no question that they increase productivity, and thus our collective wealth. But at the same time, the computer, like all general purpose technologies, requires parallel innovation in business models, organizational processes structures, institutions, and skills. These intangible assets, comprising both organizational and human capital, are often ignored on companies' balance sheets and in the official GDP statistics, but they are no less essential than hardware and software.

And that's a problem. Digital technologies change rapidly, but organizations and skills aren't keeping pace. As a result, millions of people are being left behind. Their incomes and jobs are being destroyed, leaving them worse off in absolute purchasing power than before the digital revolution. While the foundation of our economic system presumes a strong link between value creation and job creation, the Great Recession reveals the weakening or breakage of that link. This is not merely an artifact of the business cycle but rather a symptom of a deeper structural change in the nature of production. As technology accelerates on the second half of the chessboard, so will the economic mismatches, undermining our social contract and ultimately hurting both rich and poor, not just the first waves of unemployed.

The economics of technology, productivity, and employment are increasingly fodder for debate and seemingly filled with paradoxes. How can so much value creation and so much economic misfortune coexist? How can technologies accelerate while incomes stagnate? These apparent paradoxes can be resolved by combining some well-understood economic principles with the observation that there is a growing mismatch between rapidly advancing digital technologies and slow-changing humans.

Growing Productivity

Of the plethora of economic statistics—unemployment, inflation, trade, budget deficits, money supply, and so on—one is paramount: productivity growth. Productivity is the amount of output per unit of input. In particular, labor productivity can be measured as output per worker or output per hour worked. In the long run, productivity growth is almost the only thing that matters for ensuring rising living standards. Robert Solow earned his Nobel Prize for showing that economic growth does not come from people working harder but rather from working smarter. That means using new technologies and new techniques of production to create more value without increasing the labor, capital, and other resources used.

Even a few percentage points of faster productivity growth per year can lead to large differences in wealth over time. If labor productivity grows at 1%, as it did for much of the 1800s, then it takes about 70 years for living standards to double. However, if it grows at 4% per year, as it did in 2010, then living standards are 16 times higher after 70 years. While 4% growth is exceptional, the good news is that the past decade was a pretty good one for labor productivity growth—the best since the 1960s. The average of over 2.5% growth per year is far better than the 1970s and 1980s, and even edges out the 1990s (see Figure 3.1). What's more, there's now a near consensus among economists about the source of the productivity surge since the mid-1990s: IT.

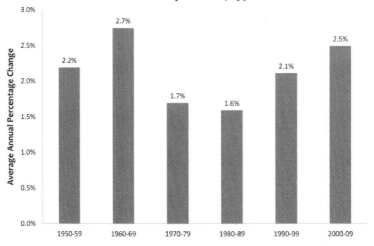

Figure 3.1: Productivity growth has been growing.
Source: Bureau of Labor Statistics.

Although the official productivity statistics are encouraging, they are far from perfect. They don't do a very good job of accounting for quality, variety, timeliness, customer service, or other hard-to-measure aspects of output. While bushels of wheat and tons of steel are relatively easy to count, the quality of a teacher's instruction, the value of more cereal choices in a supermarket, or the ability to get money from an ATM 24 hours a day is harder to assess.

Compounding this measurement problem is the fact that free digital goods like Facebook, Wikipedia, and YouTube are essentially invisible to productivity statistics. As the Internet and mobile telephony deliver more and more free services, and people spend more of their waking hours consuming them, this source of measurement error becomes increasingly important. Furthermore, most government services are simply valued at cost, which implicitly assumes zero productivity growth for this entire sector, regardless of whether true productivity is rising at levels comparable to the rest of the economy.

A final source of measurement error comes from health care, a particularly large and important segment of the economy. Health care productivity is poorly measured and often assumed to be stagnant, yet Americans live on average about 10 years longer today than they did in 1960. This is enormously valuable, but it is not counted in our productivity data. According to economist William Nordhaus, "to a first approximation, the economic value of increases in longevity over the twentieth century is about as large as the value of measured growth in non-health goods and services."

Earlier eras also had significant unmeasured quality components, such as the welfare gains from telephones, or disease reductions from antibiotics. Furthermore, there are also areas where the productivity statistics overestimate growth, as when they fail to account for increases in pollution or when increased crime leads people to spend more on crime-deterring goods and services. On balance, the official productivity data likely underestimate the true improvements of our living standards over time.

Stagnant Median Income

In contrast to labor productivity, median family income has risen only slowly since the 1970s (Figure 3.2) once the effects of inflation are taken into account. As discussed in Chapter 1, Tyler Cowen and others point to this fact as evidence of economy-wide stagnation.

Figure 3.2: Real median family income has stagnated.
Source: Bureau of Labor Statistics.

In some ways, Cowen understates his case. If you zoom in on the past decade and focus on working-age households, real median income has actually fallen from $60,746 to $55,821. This is the first decade to see declining median income since the figures were first compiled. Median net worth also declined this past decade when adjusted for inflation, another first.

Yet at the same time, GDP per person has continued to grow fairly steadily (except during recessions). The contrast with median income is striking (Figure 3.3).

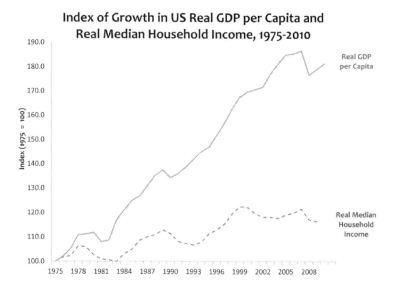

Figure 3.3: Real GDP per capita has grown significantly faster than real median household income.
Source: Bureau of Labor Statistics.

How can this be? Most of the difference stems from the distinction between the median and the mean of the distribution.[2] If 50 construction workers are drinking at a bar and Bill Gates walks in as the poorest customer walks out, the mean wealth of the customers would soar to $1 billion. However, the wealth of the median customer, the one exactly in the middle of the distribution, wouldn't change at all.

---

[2] The difference also reflects the fact that households are somewhat smaller now than in the past (thus, household income will grow less than individual income) and some technical differences between the way GDP and income are calculated.

Something like this has been happening to incomes in the U.S. economy. There have been trillions of dollars of wealth created in recent decades, but most of it went to a relatively small share of the population. In fact, economist Ed Wolff found that over 100% of all the wealth increase in America between 1983 and 2009 accrued to the top 20% of households. The other four-fifths of the population saw a net *decrease* in wealth over nearly 30 years. In turn, the top 5% accounted for over 80% of the net increase in wealth and the top 1% for over 40%. With almost a fractal-like quality, each successively finer slice at the top of the distribution accounted for a disproportionately large share of the total wealth gains. We have certainly not increased our GDP in the way that Franklin D. Roosevelt hoped for when he said during his second inaugural address in 1937, "The test of our progress is not whether we add more to the abundance of those who have much; it is whether we provide enough for those who have too little."

This squares with the evidence from Chapter 2 of the growing performance of machines. There has been no stagnation in technological progress or aggregate wealth creation as is sometimes claimed. Instead, the stagnation of median incomes primarily reflects a fundamental change in how the economy apportions income and wealth. The median worker is losing the race against the machine.

Examining other statistics reveals a deeper, more widespread problem. Not only are income and wages—the price of labor—suffering, but so is the number of jobs or the quantity of labor demanded (Figure 3.4). The last decade was the first decade since the depths of the Great Depression that saw no net job creation.

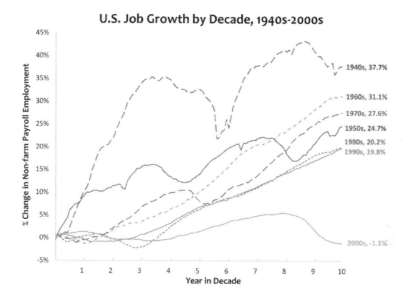

U.S. Job Growth by Decade, 1940s-2000s

Figure 3.4: In the new millennium, job growth stalls.
Source: Bureau of Labor Statistics.

When you consider that the overall population has grown, the lack of job creation is even more troubling. The population of the United States grew by 30 million in the past decade, so we would need to create 18 million jobs just to keep the same share of the population working as in the year 2000. Instead, we've created virtually none, reducing the employment to a population ratio from over 64% to barely 58%.

The lack of jobs is not simply a matter of massive layoffs due to the Great Recession. Instead, it reflects deep structural issues that have been worsening for a decade or more. The Bureau of Labor Statistics Job Openings and Labor Turnover Survey (JOLTS) shows a dramatic decrease in hiring since 2000. Lack of hiring, rather than increases in layoffs, is what accounts for most of the current joblessness. Furthermore, a study by economists Steven J. Davis, Jason Faberman, and John Haltiwanger found that recruiting intensity per job opening has plummeted during the past decade as well. Employers just don't seem to have the same demand for labor that they once did.

This reflects a pattern that was noticeable in the "jobless recovery" of the early 1990s, but that has worsened after each of the two recessions since then. Economists Menzie Chinn and Robert Gordon, in separate analyses, find that the venerable relationship between output and employment known as Okun's Law has been amended. Historically, increased output meant increased employment, but the recent recovery created much less employment than predicted; GDP rebounded but jobs didn't. The historically strong relationship between changes in GDP and changes in employment appears to have weakened as digital technology has become more pervasive and powerful. As the examples in Chapter 2 make clear, this is not a coincidence.

How Technology Can Destroy Jobs

At least since the followers of Ned Ludd smashed mechanized looms in 1811, workers have worried about automation destroying jobs. Economists have reassured them that new jobs would be created even as old ones were eliminated. For over 200 years, the economists were right. Despite massive automation of millions of jobs, more Americans had jobs at the end of each decade up through the end of the 20th century. However, this empirical fact conceals a dirty secret. There is no economic law that says that everyone, or even most people, automatically benefit from technological progress.

People with little economics training intuitively grasp this point. They understand that some human workers may lose out in the race against the machine. Ironically, the best-educated economists are often the most resistant to this idea, as the standard models of economic growth implicitly assume that economic growth benefits all residents of a country. However, just as Nobel Prize-winning economist Paul Samuelson showed that outsourcing and offshoring do not necessarily increase the welfare of all workers, it is also true that technological progress is not a rising tide that automatically raises all incomes. Even as overall wealth increases, there can be, and usually will be, winners and losers. And the losers are not necessarily some small segment of the labor force like buggy whip manufacturers. In principle, they can be a majority or even 90% or more of the population.

If wages can freely adjust, then the losers keep their jobs in exchange for accepting ever-lower compensation as technology continues to improve. But there's a limit to this adjustment. Shortly after the Luddites began smashing the machinery that they thought threatened their jobs, the economist David Ricardo, who initially thought that advances in technology would benefit all, developed an abstract model that showed the possibility of technological unemployment. The basic idea was that at some point, the equilibrium wages for workers might fall below the level needed for subsistence. A rational human would see no point in taking a job at a wage that low, so the worker would go unemployed and the work would be done by a machine instead.

Of course, this was only an abstract model. But in his book *A Farewell to Alms,* economist Gregory Clark gives an eerie real-world example of this phenomenon in action:

> There was a type of employee at the beginning of the Industrial Revolution whose job and livelihood largely vanished in the early twentieth century. This was the horse. The population of working horses actually peaked in England long after the Industrial Revolution, in 1901, when 3.25 million were at work. Though they had been replaced by rail for long-distance haulage and by steam engines for driving machinery, they still plowed fields, hauled wagons and carriages short distances, pulled boats on the canals, toiled in the pits, and carried armies into battle. But the arrival of the internal combustion engine in the late

nineteenth century rapidly displaced these workers, so that by 1924 there were fewer than two million. There was always a wage at which all these horses could have remained employed. But that wage was so low that it did not pay for their feed.

As technology continues to advance in the second half of the chessboard, taking on jobs and tasks that used to belong only to human workers, one can imagine a time in the future when more and more jobs are more cheaply done by machines than humans. And indeed, the wages of unskilled workers have trended downward for over 30 years, at least in the United States.

We also now understand that technological unemployment can occur even when wages are still well above subsistence if there are downward rigidities that prevent them from falling as quickly as advances in technology reduce the costs of automation. Minimum wage laws, unemployment insurance, health benefits, prevailing wage laws, and long-term contracts—not to mention custom and psychology—make it difficult to rapidly reduce wages.[3] Furthermore, employers will often find wage cuts damaging to morale. As the efficiency wage literature notes, such cuts can be demotivating to employees and cause companies to lose their best people.

But complete wage flexibility would be no panacea, either. Ever-falling wages for significant shares of the workforce is not exactly an appealing solution to the threat of technological employment. Aside from the damage it does to the living standards of the affected workers, lower pay only postpones the day of reckoning. Moore's Law is not a one-time blip but an accelerating exponential trend.

---

[3] Such wage rigidities have been widely observed and lie at the heart of many macroeconomic models of the business cycle.

The threat of technological unemployment is real. To understand this threat, we'll define three overlapping sets of winners and losers that technical change creates: (1) high-skilled vs. low-skilled workers, (2) superstars vs. everyone else, and (3) capital vs. labor. Each set has well-documented facts and compelling links to digital technology. What's more, these sets are not mutually exclusive. In fact, the winners in one set are more likely to be winners in the other two sets as well, which concentrates the consequences.

In each case, economic theory is clear. Even when technological progress increases productivity and overall wealth, it can also affect the division of rewards, potentially making some people worse off than they were before the innovation. In a growing economy, the gains to the winners may be larger than the losses of those who are hurt, but this is a small consolation to those who come out on the short end of the bargain.

Ultimately, the effects of technology are an empirical question— one that is best settled by looking at the data. For all three sets of winners and losers, the news is troubling. Let's look at each in turn.

1. High-Skilled vs. Low-Skilled Workers

We'll start with skill-biased technical change, which is perhaps the most carefully studied of the three phenomena. This is technical change that increases the relative demand for high-skill labor while reducing or eliminating the demand for low-skill labor. A lot of factory automation falls into this category, as routine drudgery is turned over to machines while more complex programming, management, and marketing decisions remain the purview of humans.

A recent paper by economists Daron Acemoglu and David Autor highlights the growing divergence in earnings between the most-educated and least-educated workers. Over the past 40 years, weekly wages for those with a high school degree have fallen and wages for those with a high school degree and some college have stagnated. On the other hand, college-educated workers have seen significant gains, with the biggest gains going to those who have completed graduate training (Figure 3.5).

What's more, this increase in the relative price of educated labor— their wages—comes during a period where the *supply* of educated workers has also increased. The combination of higher pay in the face of growing supply points unmistakably to an increase in the relative *demand* for skilled labor. Because those with the least education typically already had the lowest wages, this change has increased overall income inequality.

Figure 3.5: Wages have increased for those with the most education, while falling for those with the least.
Source: Acemoglu and Autor analysis of the
Current Population Survey for 1963-2008.

It's clear from the chart in Figure 3.5 that wage divergence accelerated in the digital era. As documented in careful studies by

David Autor, Lawrence Katz, and Alan Krueger, as well as Frank Levy and Richard Murnane and many others, the increase in the relative demand for skilled labor is closely correlated with advances in technology, particularly digital technologies. Hence, the moniker "skill-biased technical change," or SBTC. There are two distinct components to recent SBTC. Technologies like robotics, numerically controlled machines, computerized inventory control, and automatic transcription have been substituting for routine tasks, displacing those workers. Meanwhile other technologies like data visualization, analytics, high-speed communications, and rapid prototyping have augmented the contributions of more abstract and data-driven reasoning, increasing the value of those jobs.

Skill-biased technical change has also been important in the past. For most of the 19th century, about 25% of all agriculture labor threshed grain. That job was automated in the 1860s. The 20th century was marked by an accelerating mechanization not only of agriculture but also of factory work. Echoing the first Nobel Prize winner in economics, Jan Tinbergen, Harvard economists Claudia Goldin and Larry Katz described the resulting SBTC as a "race between education and technology." Ever-greater investments in education, dramatically increasing the average educational level of the American workforce, helped prevent inequality from soaring as technology automated more and more unskilled work. While education is certainly not synonymous with skill, it is one of the most easily measurable correlates of skill, so this pattern suggests that demand for upskilling has increased faster than its supply.

Studies by this book's co-author Erik Brynjolfsson along with Timothy Bresnahan, Lorin Hitt, and Shinku Yang found that a key aspect of SBTC was not just the skills of those working with computers, but more importantly the broader changes in work organization that were made possible by information technology. The most productive firms reinvented and reorganized decision rights, incentives systems, information flows, hiring systems, and other aspects of organizational capital to get the most from the technology. This, in turn, required radically different and, generally, higher skill levels in the workforce. It was not so much that those directly working with computers had to be more skilled, but rather that whole production processes, and even industries, were reengineered to exploit powerful new information technologies. What's more, each dollar of computer hardware was often the catalyst for more than $10 of investment in complementary organizational capital. The intangible organizational assets are typically much harder to change, but they are also much more important to the success of the organization.

As the 21st century unfolds, automation is affecting broader swaths of work. Even the low wages earned by factory workers in China have not insulated them from being undercut by new machinery and the complementary organizational and institutional changes. For instance, Terry Gou, the founder and chairman of the electronics manufacturer Foxconn, announced this year a plan to purchase 1 million robots over the next three years to replace much of his workforce. The robots will take over routine jobs like spraying paint, welding, and basic assembly. Foxconn currently has 10,000 robots, with 300,000 expected to be in place by next year.

2. Superstars vs. Everyone Else

The second division is between superstars and everyone else. Many industries are winner-take-all or winner-take-most competitions, in which a few individuals get the lion's share of the rewards. Think of pop music, professional athletics, and the market for CEOs. Digital technologies increase the size and scope of these markets. These technologies replicate not only information goods but increasingly business processes as well. As a result, the talents, insights, or decisions of a single person can now dominate a national or even global market. Meanwhile good, but not great, local competitors are increasingly crowded out of their markets. The superstars in each field can now earn much larger rewards than they did in earlier decades.

The effects are evident at the top of the income distribution. The top 10% of the wage distribution has done much better than the rest of the labor force, but even within this group there has been growing inequality. Income has grown faster for the top 1% than the rest of the top decile. In turn, the top 0.1% and top 0.01% have seen their income grow even faster. This is not run-of-the-mill skill-biased technical change but rather reflects the unique rewards of superstardom. Sherwin Rosen, himself a superstar economist, laid out the economics of superstars in a seminal 1981 article. In many markets, consumers are willing to pay a premium for the very best. If technology exists for a single seller to cheaply replicate his or her services, then the top-quality provider can capture most—or all—of the market. The next-best provider might be almost as good yet get only a tiny fraction of the revenue.

Technology can convert an ordinary market into one that is characterized by superstars. Before the era of recorded music, the very best singer might have filled a large concert hall but at most would only be able to reach thousands of listeners over the course of a year. Each city might have its own local stars, with a few top performers touring nationally, but even the best singer in the nation could reach only a relatively small fraction of the potential listening audience. Once music could be recorded and distributed at a very low marginal cost, however, a small number of top performers could capture the majority of revenues in every market, from classical music's Yo-Yo Ma to pop's Lady Gaga.

Economists Robert Frank and Philip Cook documented how winner-take-all markets have proliferated as technology transformed not only recorded music but also software, drama, sports, and every other industry that can be transmitted as digital bits. This trend has accelerated as more of the economy is based on software, either implicitly or explicitly. As we discussed in our 2008 *Harvard Business Review* article, digital technologies make it possible to replicate not only bits but also processes. For instance, companies like CVS have embedded processes like prescription drug ordering into their enterprise information systems. Each time CVS makes an improvement, it is propagated across 4,000 stores nationwide, amplifying its value. As a result, the reach and impact of an executive decision, like how to organize a process, is correspondingly larger.

In fact, the ratio of CEO pay to average worker pay has increased from 70 in 1990 to 300 in 2005, and much of this growth is linked to the greater use of IT, according to recent research that Erik did with his student Heekyung Kim. They found that increases in the compensation of other top executives followed a similar, if less extreme, pattern. Aided by digital technologies, entrepreneurs, CEOs, entertainment stars, and financial executives have been able to leverage their talents across global markets and capture reward that would have been unimaginable in earlier times.

To be sure, technology is not the only factor that affects incomes. Political factors, globalization, changes in asset prices, and, in the case of CEOs and financial executives, corporate governance also plays a role. In particular, the financial services sector has grown dramatically as a share of GDP and even more as a share of profits and compensation, especially at the top of the income distribution. While efficient finance is essential to a modern economy, it appears that a significant share of returns to large human and technological investments in the past decade, such as those in sophisticated computerized program trading, were from rent redistribution rather than genuine wealth creation. Other countries, with different institutions and also slower adoption of IT, have seen less extreme changes in inequality. But the overall changes in the United States have been substantial. According to economist Emmanuel Saez, the top 1% of U.S. households got 65% of all the growth in the economy since 2002. In fact, Saez reports that the top 0.01% of households in the United States—that is, the 14,588 families with income above $11,477,000—saw their share of national income double from 3% to 6% between 1995 and 2007.

3. Capital vs. Labor

The third division is between capital and labor. Most types of production require both machinery and human labor. According to bargaining theory, the wealth they generate is divided according to relative bargaining power, which in turn typically reflects the contribution of each input. If the technology decreases the relative importance of human labor in a particular production process, the owners of capital equipment will be able to capture a bigger share of income from the goods and services produced. To be sure, capital owners are also humans—so it's not like the wealth disappears from society—but capital owners are typically a very different and smaller group than the ones doing most of the labor, so the distribution of income will be affected.

In particular, if technology replaces labor, you might expect that the shares of income earned by equipment owners would rise relative to laborers—the classic bargaining battle between capital and labor.[4] This has been happening increasingly in recent years. As noted by Kathleen Madigan, since the recession ended, real spending on equipment and software has soared by 26% while payrolls have remained essentially flat.

Furthermore, there is growing evidence that capital has captured a growing share of GDP in recent years. As shown in Figure 3.6, corporate profits have easily surpassed their pre-recession levels.

---

[4] The precise economic theory is a bit more complicated, however. In a well-functioning market, rewards for capital (or labor) tend to reflect the value of an additional piece of capital (or additional worker) *at the margin*. Depending on how expensive it is to increase the capital stock, the rewards earned by capitalists may not automatically grow with increased automation—the predicted effects depend on the exact details of the production, distribution, and governance systems.

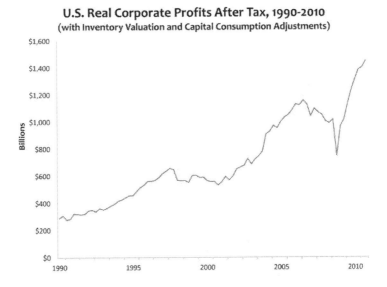

Figure 3.6: Profits soar in the current recovery.
Source: Bureau of Economic Analysis.

According to the recently updated data from the U.S. Commerce Department, recent corporate profits accounted for 23.8% of total domestic corporate income, a record high share that is more than 1 full percentage point above the previous record. Similarly, corporate profits as a share of GDP are at 50-year highs. Meanwhile, compensation to labor in all forms, including wages and benefits, is at a 50-year low. Capital is getting a bigger share of the pie, relative to labor.

The recession exacerbated this trend, but it's part of long-term change in the economy. As noted by economists Susan Fleck, John Glaser, and Shawn Sprague, the trend line for labor's share of GDP was essentially flat between 1974 and 1983 but has been falling since then. When one thinks about the workers in places like Foxconn's factory being replaced by labor-saving robots, it's easy to imagine a technology-driven story for why the relative shares of income might be changing.

It's important to note that the "labor" share in the Bureau of Labor Statistics' data includes wages paid to CEOs, finance professionals, professional athletes, and other "superstars" discussed above. In this sense, the declining labor share understates how badly the median worker has fared. It may also understate the division of income between capital and labor, insofar as CEOs and other top executives may have bargaining power to capture some of the "capital's share" that would otherwise accrue to owners of common stock.

Inequality Can Affect the Overall Size of the Economy

Technology changes the shares of income for the skilled vs. unskilled, for superstars vs. the rest, and for capital vs. labor. Is this simply a zero-sum game where the losses of some are exactly offset by gains to others? Not necessarily. On the positive side of the ledger, inequality can provide beneficial incentives for skill acquisition, efforts toward superstardom, or capital accumulation. However, there are also several ways it can hurt economic well-being.

First, one of the most basic regularities of economics is the declining marginal utility of income. A $1,000 windfall is likely to increase your happiness, or utility, less if you already have $10 million than if you only have $10,000. Second, equality of opportunity is important to the efficiency and fairness of a society, even if unequal outcomes are tolerated or even celebrated. Equality of opportunity, however, can be harder to achieve if children of poverty get inadequate health care, nutrition, or education, or people at the bottom are otherwise unable to compete on a level-playing field. Third, inequality inevitably affects politics, and this can be damaging and destabilizing. As economist Daron Acemoglu puts it:

> Economic power tends to beget political power even in democratic and pluralistic societies. In the United States,

47

this tends to work through campaign contributions and access to politicians that wealth and money tend to buy. This political channel implies another, potentially more powerful and distortionary link between inequality and a non-level playing field.

Finally, when technology leads to relatively sudden shifts in income between groups, it may also dampen overall economic growth and potentially precipitate the kind of collapse in aggregate demand reflected in the current slump.

Consider each of the three sets of winners and losers discussed earlier. When SBTC increases the incomes of high-skill workers and decreases the incomes and employment of low-skill workers, the net effect may be a fall in overall demand. High-skill workers, given extra income, may choose to increase their leisure and savings rather than work extra hours. Meanwhile, low-skill workers lose their jobs, go on disability, or otherwise drop out of the labor force. Both groups work less than before, so overall output falls.[5]

One can tell a similar story for how super-wealthy superstars, given additional wealth, choose to save most of it while their less-than-stellar competitors have to cut back consumption. Again, overall output falls from such a shift. Former secretary of labor Robert Reich has argued that such a dynamic was in part responsible for the Great Depression, and Nobel Prize winner Joseph Stiglitz has written in detail about how the increasing concentration of wealth in a relatively small group can be corrosive to economic growth.

Finally, it's easy to see how a shift in income from labor to capital would lead to a similar reduction in overall demand. Capitalists tend to save more of each marginal dollar than laborers. In the short run, a transfer from laborers to capitalists reduces total consumption, and thus total GDP. This phenomenon is summarized in a classic though possibly apocryphal story: Ford

---

[5] Economist Arnold Kling describes such a model on his blog.

CEO Henry Ford II and United Automobile Workers president Walter Reuther are jointly touring a modern auto plant. Ford jokingly jabs at Reuther: "Walter, how are you going to get these robots to pay UAW dues?" Not missing a beat, Reuther responds: "Henry, how are you going to get them to buy your cars?"

Over time, a well-functioning economy should be able to adjust to the new consumption path required by any or all of these types of reallocations of income. For instance, about 90% of Americans worked in agriculture in 1800; by 1900 it was 41%, and by 2000 it was just 2%. As workers left farms over the course of two centuries, there were more than enough new jobs created in other sectors, and whole new industries sprang up to employ them. However, when the changes happen faster than expectations and/or institutions can adjust, the transition can be cataclysmic. Accelerating technology in the past decade has disrupted not just one sector but virtually all of them. A common way to maintain consumption temporarily in the face of an adverse shock is to borrow more. While this is feasible in the short run, and is even rational if the shock is expected to be temporary, it is unsustainable if the trend continues or, worse, grows in magnitude.

Arguably, something like this has happened in the past decade. Wages for many Americans fell well short of historical growth rates and even fell in real terms for many groups as technology transformed their industries. Borrowing helped mask the problem until the Great Recession came along. The gradual demand collapse that might have been spread over decades was compressed into a much shorter period, making it harder for workers to change their skills, entrepreneurs to invent new business models, and managers to make the necessary adjustments equally quickly. The result has been a dysfunctional series of crises. Certainly, much of the recent unemployment is, as past business cycles, simply due to weak demand in the overall economy, reflecting an extremely severe downturn. However, this does not negate the important structural component to the falling levels of employment, and it is plausible that the Great Recession itself may, in part, reflect a delayed response to these deeper structural issues.

Looking Ahead

As we look ahead, we see these three trends not only accelerating but also evolving. For instance, new research by David Autor and David Dorn has put an interesting twist on the SBTC story. They find that the relationship between skills and wages has recently become U-shaped. In the most recent decade, demand has fallen most for those in the middle of the skill distribution. The highest-skilled workers have done well, but interestingly those with the lowest skills have suffered less than those with average skills, reflecting a polarization of labor demand.

This reflects an interesting fact about automation. It can be easier to automate the work of a bookkeeper, bank teller, or semi-skilled factory worker than a gardener, hairdresser, or home health aide. In particular, over the past 25 years, physical activities that require a degree of physical coordination and sensory perception have proven more resistant to automation than basic information processing, a phenomenon known as Moravec's Paradox. For instance, many types of clerical work have been automated, and millions of people interact with robot bank tellers and airport ticket agents each day. More recently, call center work—which was widely offshored to India, the Philippines, or other low-wage nations in the 1990s—has increasingly been replaced by automated voice response systems that can recognize an increasingly large domain-specific vocabulary and even complete sentences.

In contrast, vision, fine motor skills, and locomotion have been much harder to automate. The human brain can draw on highly specialized neural circuitry, refined by millions of years of evolution, to recognize faces, manipulate objects, and walk through unstructured environments. Although multiplying five-digit numbers is an unnatural and difficult skill for the human mind to master, the visual cortex routinely does far more complex mathematics each time it detects an edge or uses parallax to locate an object in space. Machine computation has surpassed humans in the first task but not yet in the second one.

As digital technologies continue to improve, we are skeptical that even these skills will remain bastions of human exceptionalism in the coming decades. The examples in Chapter 2 of Google's self-driving car and IBM's Watson point to a different path going forward. The technology is rapidly emerging to automate truck driving in the coming decade, just as scheduling truck routes was increasingly automated in the last decade. Likewise, the high end of the skill spectrum is also vulnerable, as we see in the case of e-discovery displacing lawyers and, perhaps, in a Watson-like technology, displacing human medical diagnosticians.

Some Conclusions

Technology has advanced rapidly, and the good news is that this has radically increased the economy's productive capacity. However, technological progress does not automatically benefit everyone in a society. In particular, incomes have become more uneven, as have employment opportunities. Recent technological advances have favored some skill groups over others, particularly "superstars" in many fields, and probably also increased the overall share of GDP accruing to capital relative to labor.

The stagnation in median income is not because of a lack of technological progress. On the contrary, the problem is that our skills and institutions have not kept up with the rapid changes in technology. In the 19th and 20th centuries, as each successive wave of automation eliminated jobs in some sectors and occupations, entrepreneurs identified new opportunities where labor could be redeployed and workers learned the necessary skills to succeed. Millions of people left agriculture, but an even larger number found employment in manufacturing and services.

In the 21st century, technological change is both faster and more pervasive. While the steam engine, electric motor, and internal combustion engine were each impressive technologies, they were not subject to an ongoing level of continuous improvement anywhere near the pace seen in digital technologies. Already, computers are thousands of times more powerful than they were 30 years ago, and all evidence suggests that this pace will continue for at least another decade, and probably more. Furthermore, computers are, in some sense, the "universal machine" that has applications in almost all industries and tasks. In particular, digital technologies now perform mental tasks that had been the exclusive domain of humans in the past. General purpose computers are directly relevant not only to the 60% of the labor force involved in information processing tasks but also to more and more of the remaining 40%. As the technology moves into the second half of the chessboard, each successive doubling in power will increase the number of applications where it can affect work and employment. As a result, our skills and institutions will have to work harder and harder to keep up lest more and more of the labor force faces technological unemployment.

CHAPTER 4.
WHAT IS TO BE DONE?
PRESCRIPTIONS AND
RECOMMENDATIONS

The greatest task before civilization at present is to make machines what they ought to be, the slaves, instead of the masters of men.

— Havelock Ellis, 1922

In the previous two chapters we showed how quickly and deeply computers are encroaching into human territory, and discussed the economic consequences of this phenomenon—how digital progress can leave some people worse off even as it improves productivity and grows the overall pie. Of course, concerns about the interplay between technology and economics are not new. In fact, they've even entered American folklore.

The legend of John Henry became popular in the late 19th century as the effects of the steam-powered Industrial Revolution affected every industry and job that relied heavily on human strength. It's the story of a contest between a steam drill and John Henry, a powerful railroad worker, to see which of the two could bore the longer hole into solid rock.[6] Henry wins this race against the machine but loses his life; his exertions cause his heart to burst. Humans never directly challenged the steam drill again.

---

[6] Railroad construction crews of the time blasted tunnels through mountainsides by drilling holes into the rock, packing the holes with explosives, and detonating them.

This legend reflected popular unease at the time about the potential for technology to make human labor obsolete. But this is not at all what happened as the Industrial Revolution progressed. As steam power advanced and spread throughout industry, more human workers were needed, not fewer. They were needed not for their raw physical strength (as was the case with John Henry) but instead for other human skills: physical ones like locomotion, dexterity, coordination, and perception, and mental ones like communication, pattern matching, and creativity.

The John Henry legend shows us that, in many contexts, humans will eventually lose the head-to-head race against the machine. But the broader lesson of the first Industrial Revolution is more like the Indy 500 than John Henry: economic progress comes from constant innovation in which people race *with* machines. Human and machine collaborate together in a race to produce more, to capture markets, and to beat other teams of humans and machines.

This lesson remains valid and instructive today as machines are winning head-to-head mental contests, not just physical ones. Here again, we observe that things get really interesting once this contest is over and people start racing with machines instead of against them.

The game of chess provides a great example. In 1997, Gary Kasparov, humanity's most brilliant chess master, lost to Deep Blue, a $10 million specialized supercomputer programmed by a team from IBM. That was big news when it happened, but then developments in the world of chess went back to being reported on and read mainly by chess geeks. As a result, it's not well known that the best chess player on the planet today is not a computer. Nor is it a human. The best chess player is a team of humans using computers.

After head-to-head matches between humans and computers became uninteresting (because the computers always won), the action moved to "freestyle" competitions, allowing any combination of people and machines. The overall winner in a recent freestyle tournament had neither the best human players nor the most powerful computers. As Kasparov writes, it instead consisted of

> a pair of amateur American chess players using three computers at the same time. Their skill at manipulating and "coaching" their computers to look very deeply into positions effectively counteracted the superior chess understanding of their grandmaster opponents and the greater computational power of other participants. ... Weak human + machine + better process was superior to a strong computer alone and, more remarkably, superior to a strong human + machine + inferior process.

This pattern is true not only in chess but throughout the economy. In medicine, law, finance, retailing, manufacturing, and even scientific discovery, the key to winning the race is not to compete *against* machines but to compete *with* machines. As we saw in Chapter 2, while computers win at routine processing, repetitive arithmetic, and error-free consistency and are quickly getting better at complex communication and pattern matching, they lack intuition and creativity and are lost when asked to work even a little outside a predefined domain. Fortunately, humans are strongest exactly where computers are weak, creating a potentially beautiful partnership.

As this partnership advances, we're not too worried about computers holding up their end of the bargain. Technologists are doing an amazing job of making them ever faster, smaller, more energy efficient, and cheaper over time. We are confident that these trends will continue even as we move deeper into the second half of the chessboard.

Digital progress, in fact, is so rapid and relentless that people and organizations are having a hard time keeping up. So in this chapter we want to focus on recommendations in two areas: improving the rate and quality of organizational innovation, and increasing human capital—ensuring that people have the skills they need to participate in today's economy, and tomorrow's. Making progress in these two areas will be the best way to allow human workers and institutions to race with machines, not against them.

Fostering Organizational Innovation

How can we implement a "race with machines" strategy? The solution is organizational innovation: co-inventing new organizational structures, processes, and business models that leverage ever-advancing technology and human skills. Joseph Schumpeter, the economist, described this as a process of "creative destruction" and gave entrepreneurs the central role in the development and propagation of the necessary innovations. Entrepreneurs reap rich rewards because what they do, when they do it well, is both incredibly valuable and far too rare.

To put it another way, the stagnation of median wages and polarization of job growth is an *opportunity* for creative entrepreneurs. They can develop new business models that combine the swelling numbers of mid-skilled workers with ever-cheaper technology to create value. There has never been a worse time to be competing with machines, but there has never been a better time to be a talented entrepreneur.

Entrepreneurial energy in America's tech sector drove the most visible reinvention of the economy. Google, Facebook, Apple, and Amazon, among others, have created hundreds of billions of dollars of shareholder value by creating whole new product categories, ecosystems, and even industries. New platforms leverage technology to create marketplaces that address the employment crisis by bringing together machines and human skills in new and unexpected ways:

- eBay and Amazon Marketplace spurred over 600,000 people to earn their livings by dreaming up new, improved, or simply different or cheaper products for a worldwide customer base. The Long Tail of new products offered enormous consumer value and is a rapidly growing segment of the economy.

- Apple's App Store and Google's Android Marketplace make it easy for people with ideas for mobile applications to create and distribute them.

- Threadless lets people create and sell designs for t-shirts. Amazon's Mechanical Turk makes it easy to find cheap labor to do a breathtaking array of simple, well-defined tasks. Kickstarter flips this model on its head and helps designers and creative artists find sponsors for their projects.

- Heartland Robotics provides cheap robots-in-a-box that make it possible for small business people to quickly set up their own highly automated factory, dramatically reducing the costs and increasing the flexibility of manufacturing.

Collectively, these new businesses directly create millions of new jobs.[7] Some of them also create platforms for thousands of other entrepreneurs. None of them may ever create billion-dollar

---

[7] It's also worth noting that some valuable enterprises need not create paying jobs to generate value in the economy. For instance, Wikipedia thrives on a model that is largely separate from the financial economy, but it nonetheless provides rewards and value. Judging by the revealed preferences of participants, Wikipedia provides sufficient non-monetary rewards to attract millions of contributors with diverse talents and expertise who create tremendous value. When thinking about the evolving economy, we need to remember that Abraham Maslow's hierarchy of needs extends beyond material things.

businesses themselves, but collectively they can do more to create jobs and wealth than even the most successful single venture.

As the great theorist of markets Friedrich Hayek noted, some of the most valuable knowledge in an economy is dispersed among individuals. It is

> the knowledge of the particular circumstances of time and place. ... To know of and put to use a machine not fully employed, or somebody's skill which could be better utilized, or to be aware of a surplus stock which can be drawn upon during an interruption of supplies, is socially quite as useful as the knowledge of better alternative techniques. And the shipper who earns his living from using otherwise empty or half-filled journeys of tramp-steamers, or the estate agent whose whole knowledge is almost exclusively one of temporary opportunities, or the arbitrageur who gains from local differences of commodity prices, are all performing eminently useful functions based on special knowledge of circumstances of the fleeting moment not known to others.

Fortunately, digital technologies create enormous opportunities for individuals to use their unique and dispersed knowledge for the benefit of the whole economy. As a result, technology enables more and more opportunities for what Google chief economist Hal Varian calls "micromultinationals"—businesses with less than a dozen employees that sell to customers worldwide and often draw on worldwide supplier and partner networks. While the archetypal 20th-century multinational was one of a small number of megafirms with huge fixed costs and thousands of employees, the coming century will give birth to thousands of small multinationals with low fixed costs and a small number of employees each. Both models can conceivably employ similar numbers of people overall, but the latter one is likely to be more flexible.

But are there enough opportunities for all these entrepreneurs? Are we running out of innovations?

When businesses are based on bits instead of atoms, then each new product adds to the set of building blocks available to the next entrepreneur instead of depleting the stock of ideas the way minerals or farmlands are depleted in the physical world. New digital businesses are often recombinations, or mash-ups, of previous ones. For example, a student in one of our classes at MIT created a simple Facebook application for sharing photos. Although he had little formal training in programming, he created a robust and professional-looking app in a few days using standard tools. Within a year he had over 1 million users. This was possible because his innovation leveraged the Facebook user base, which in turn leveraged the broader World Wide Web, which in turn leveraged the Internet protocols, which in turn leveraged the cheap computers of Moore's Law and many other innovations. He could not have created value for his million users without the existence of these prior inventions. Because the process of innovation often relies heavily on the combining and recombining of previous innovations, the broader and deeper the pool of accessible ideas and individuals, the more opportunities there are for innovation.

We are in no danger of running out of new combinations to try. Even if technology froze today, we have more possible ways of configuring the different applications, machines, tasks, and distribution channels to create new processes and products than we could ever exhaust.

Here's a simple proof: suppose the people in a small company write down their work tasks— one task per card. If there were only 52 tasks in the company, as many as in a standard deck of cards, then there would be *52!* different ways to arrange these tasks.[8] This is far

---

[8] 52! is shorthand for 52 x 51 x 50 x ... x 2 x 1, which multiplies to over 8.06×10^{67}. That is about the number of atoms in our galaxy.

more than the number of grains of rice on the second 32 squares of a chessboard or even a second or third full chessboard. Combinatorial explosion is one of the few mathematical functions that outgrows an exponential trend. And that means that combinatorial innovation is the best way for human ingenuity to stay in the race with Moore's Law.

Most of the combinations may be no better than what we already have, but some surely will be, and a few will be "home runs" that are vast improvements. The trick is finding the ones that make a positive difference. Parallel experimentation by millions of entrepreneurs is the best and fastest way to do that. As Thomas Edison once said when trying to find the right combination of materials for a working lightbulb: "I have not failed. I've just found 10,000 ways that won't work." Multiply that by 10 million entrepreneurs and you can begin to see the scale of the economy's innovation potential. Most of this potential remains untapped.

As technology makes it possible for more people to start enterprises on a national or even global scale, more people will be in the position to earn superstar compensation. While winner-take-all economics can lead to vastly disproportionate rewards to the top performer in each market, the key is that there is no automatic ceiling to the number of different markets that can be created. In principle, tens of millions of people could each be a leading performer—even the top expert—in tens of millions of distinct, value-creating fields. Think of them as micro-experts for macro-markets. Technology scholar Thomas Malone calls this the age of hyperspecialization. Digital technologies make it possible to scale that expertise so that we all benefit from those talents and creativity.

Investing in Human Capital

Technology races ahead ever faster as we move deeper into the second half of the chessboard. To keep up, we need not only organizational innovation, orchestrated by entrepreneurs, but also a second broad strategy: investments in the complementary human capital—the education and skills required to get the most out of our racing technology. Smart entrepreneurs can, and will, invent ways to create value by employing even less skilled workers. However, the message the labor market is clearly sending is that it's much easier to create value with highly educated workers.

Unfortunately, our educational progress has stalled and, as discussed in Chapter 3, this is reflected in stagnating wages and fewer jobs. The median worker is not keeping up with cutting-edge technologies. Although the United States once led the world in the education of its citizens, it has fallen from first to tenth in the share of citizens who are college graduates. The high costs and low performance of the American educational system are classic symptoms of low productivity in this sector. Despite the importance of productivity to overall living standards, and the disproportionate importance of education to productivity, there is far too little systematic work done to measure, let alone improve, the productivity of education itself.

It's not a coincidence that the educational sector also lags as an adopter of information technologies. Basic instructional methods, involving a teacher lecturing to rows of passive students, have changed little in centuries. As the old joke goes, it's a system for transmitting information from the notes of the lecturer to the notes of the student without going through the brain of either. In many classrooms, the main instructional technology is literally a piece of yellowish limestone rock scraped across a larger black slate.

The optimistic interpretation is that we have tremendous upside potential for improvements in education. As education becomes increasingly digitized, educators can experiment and track alternative approaches, measure and identify what works, share their findings, and replicate the best approaches in other subjects and geographies. This enables a faster pace of innovation, leading to further improvements in educational productivity. It also enables unbundling of instruction, evaluation, and certification, which encourages educational systems to be based more on delivering genuine, measurable results and less on simply signaling selection, effort, and prestige.

Furthermore, using IT, both scale and customization can be increased dramatically. A good example is the free online course on artificial intelligence at Stanford that attracted at least 58,000 students. The course uses digital networks to broadcast material and track all students individually, radically improving the productivity of the instructors, lowering costs to students, and, at least in principle, delivering a quality product that would otherwise be inaccessible to the vast majority of the participants. MIT has been running similar, albeit smaller, classes using a combination of information and communication technologies for over a decade, most notably in its System Design and Management program. Students at companies around the world use a combination of information and communication technologies to interact with professors centrally located at MIT and with instructors local to each group of students.

At the K-12 level, Khan Academy offers over 2,600 short educational videos and 144 self-assessment modules for free on the web. Students can learn at their own pace, pausing and replaying videos as needed, earning "badges" to demonstrate mastery of various skills and knowledge, and charting their own curricula through the ever-growing collection of modules. Students have logged over 70 million visits to Khan Academy so far. A growing infrastructure makes it easy for parents or teachers to track student progress.

An increasingly common approach uses the Khan Academy's tools to flip the traditional classroom model on its head, letting students watch the video lectures at home at their own pace and then having them do the "home work" exercises in class while a teacher circulates among them, helping each student individually with specific difficulties rather than providing a one-size-fits-all lecture to all the students simultaneously.

Combining videoconferencing, software, and networks with local teachers and tutors has a number of potential advantages. The very best "superstar" teachers can be "replicated" via technology, giving more students a chance to learn from them. Furthermore, students can learn at their own pace. For instance, software can sense when students are having difficulties and need more detail, repetition, and perhaps a slower pace, as well as when they are quickly grasping the content and can be accelerated. Local human teachers, tutors, and peer tutoring can easily be incorporated into the system to provide some of the kinds of value that the technology can't do well, such as emotional support and less-structured instruction and assessment.

For instance, creative writing, arts instruction, and other "soft skills" are not always as amenable to rule-based software or distance learning. We concur with Rhode Island School of Design president John Maeda's vision that a move from STEM (Science, Technology, Engineering, and Mathematics) to STEAM (adding Arts to the mix) is the right vision for boosting innovation. The technology and systems for education have to be compatible with that vision.

In particular, softer skills like leadership, team building, and creativity will be increasingly important. They are the areas least likely to be automated and most in demand in a dynamic, entrepreneurial economy. Conversely, college graduates who seek the traditional type of job, where someone else tells them what to do each day, will find themselves increasingly in competition with machines, which excel at following detailed instructions.

The Limits to Organizational Innovation and Human Capital Investment

We're encouraged by the emerging opportunities to combine digital, organizational, and human capital to create wealth: technology, entrepreneurship, and education are an extraordinarily powerful combination. But we want to stress that even this combination cannot solve all our problems.

First, not everyone can or should be an entrepreneur, and not everyone can or should spend 16 or more years in school. Second, there are limits to the power of American entrepreneurship for job creation. A 2011 research report for the Kauffman Foundation by E. J. Reddy and Robert Litan found that even though the total number of new businesses founded annually in the United States has remained largely steady, the total number of people employed by them at startup has been declining in recent years. This could be because modern business technology lets a company start leaner and stay leaner as it grows.

Third, and most importantly, even when humans are racing using machines instead of against them, there are still winners and losers as described in Chapter 3. Some people, perhaps even a lot, can continue to see their incomes stagnate or shrink and their jobs vanish while overall growth continues.

When significant numbers of people see their standards of living fall despite an ever-growing economic pie, it threatens the social contract of the economy and even the social fabric of society. One instinctual response is to simply redistribute income to those who have been hurt. While redistribution ameliorates the material costs of inequality, and that's not a bad thing, it doesn't address the root of the problems our economy is facing. By itself, redistribution does nothing to make unemployed workers productive again. Furthermore, the value of gainful work is far more than the money earned. There is also the psychological value that almost all people place on doing something useful. Forced idleness is not the same as voluntary leisure. Franklin D. Roosevelt put this most eloquently:

> No country, however rich, can afford the waste of its human resources. Demoralization caused by vast unemployment is our greatest extravagance. Morally, it is the greatest menace to our social order.

Thus, we focus our recommendations on creating ways for everyone to contribute productively to the economy. As technology continues to race ahead, it can widen the gaps between the swift and the slow on many dimensions. Organizational and institutional innovations can recombine human capital with machines to create broad-based productivity growth. That's where we focus our recommendations.

Toward an Agenda for Action

By first diagnosing the reason for stagnating median income, we are in a position to prescribe solutions. These involve accelerating organizational innovation and human capital creation to keep pace with technology. There are at least 19 specific steps we can take to these ends.

Education

1. Invest in education. Start by simply paying teachers more so that more of the best and the brightest sign up for this profession, as they do in many other nations. American teachers make 40% less than the average college graduate. Teachers are some of America's most important wealth creators. Increasing the quantity and quality of skilled labor provides a double win by boosting economic growth and reducing income inequality.

2. Hold teachers accountable for performance by, for example, eliminating tenure. This should be part of the bargain for higher pay.

3. Separate student instruction from testing and certification. Focus schooling more on verifiable outcomes and measurable performance and less on signaling time, effort or prestige.

4. Keep K-12 students in classrooms for more hours. One reason American students lag behind international competitors is they simply receive about one month less instruction per year.

5. Increase the ratio of skilled workers in the United States by encouraging skilled immigrants. Offer green cards to foreign students when they complete advanced degrees, especially in science and engineering subjects at approved universities. Expand the H-1B visa program. Skilled workers in America often create more value when working with other skilled workers. Bringing them together can increase worldwide innovation and growth.

Entrepreneurship

6. Teach entrepreneurship as a skill not just in elite business schools but throughout higher education. Foster a broader class of mid-tech, middle-class entrepreneurs by training them in the fundamentals of business creation and management.

7. Boost entrepreneurship in American by creating a category of founders' visas for entrepreneurs, like those in Canada and other countries.

8. Create clearinghouses and databases to facilitate the creation and dissemination of templates for new businesses. A set of standardized packages for startups can smooth the path for new entrepreneurs in many industries. These can range from franchise opportunities to digital "cookbooks" that provide the skeleton structure for an operation. Job training should be supplemented with entrepreneurship guidance as the nature of work evolves.

9. Aggressively lower the governmental barriers to business creation. In too many industries, elaborate regulatory approvals are needed from multiple agencies at multiple levels of government. These too often have the implicit goal of preserving rents of existing business owners at the expense of new businesses and their employees.

Investment

10. Invest to upgrade the country's communications and transportation infrastructure. The American Society of Civil Engineers gives a grade of D to our overall infrastructure at present. Improving it will bring productivity benefits by facilitating flow and mixing ideas, people, and technologies. It will also put many people to work directly. You don't have to be an ardent Keynesian to believe that the best time to make these investments is when there is plenty of slack in the labor market.

11. Increase funding for basic research and for our preeminent government R&D institutions including the National Science Foundation, the National Institutes of Health, and the Defense Advanced Research Projects Agency (DARPA) with a renewed focus on intangible assets and business innovation. Like other forms of basic research, these investments are often underfunded by private investors because of the spillovers they create.

Laws, Regulations, and Taxes

12. Preserve the relative flexibility of American labor markets by resisting efforts to regulate hiring and firing. Banning layoffs paradoxically can lower employment by making it riskier for firms to hire in the first place, especially if they are experimenting with new products or business models.

13. Make it comparatively more attractive to hire a person than to buy more technology. This can be done by, among other things, decreasing employer payroll taxes and providing subsidies or tax breaks for employing people who have been out of work for a long time. Taxes on congestion and pollution can more than make up for the reduced labor taxes.

14. Decouple benefits from jobs to increase flexibility and dynamism. Tying health care and other mandated benefits to jobs makes it harder for people to move to new jobs or to quit and start new businesses. For instance, many a potential entrepreneur has been blocked by the need to maintain health insurance. Denmark and the Netherlands have led the way here.

15. Don't rush to regulate new network businesses. Some observers feel that "crowdsourcing" businesses like Amazon's Mechanical Turk exploit their members, who should therefore be better protected. However, especially in this early, experimental period, the developers of these innovative platforms should be given maximum freedom to innovate and experiment, and their members' freely made decisions to participate should be honored, not overturned.

16. Eliminate or reduce the massive home mortgage subsidy. This costs over $130 billion per year, which would do much more for growth if allocated to research or education. While home ownership has many laudable benefits, it likely *reduces* labor mobility and economic flexibility, which conflicts with the economy's increased need for flexibility.

17. Reduce the large implicit and explicit subsidies to financial services. This sector attracts a disproportionate number of the best and the brightest minds and technologies, in part because the government effectively guarantees "too big to fail" institutions.

18. Reform the patent system. Not only does it take years to issue good patents due to the backlog and shortage of qualified examiners, but too many low-quality patents are issued, clogging our courts. As a result, patent trolls are chilling innovation rather than encouraging it.

19. Shorten, rather than lengthen, copyright periods and increase the flexibility of fair use. Copyright covers too much digital content. Rather than encouraging innovation, as specified in the Constitution, excessive restrictions like the Sonny Bono Copyright Term Extension Act inhibit mixing and matching of content and using it creatively in new ways.

These suggestions are only the tip of the iceberg of a broader transformation that we need to support, not only to mitigate technological unemployment and inequality, but also to fulfill the potential for new technologies to grow the economy and create broad-based value. We are not putting forth a complete blueprint for the next economy—that task is inherently impossible. Instead, we seek to initiate a conversation. That conversation will be successful if we accurately diagnose the mismatch between accelerating technologies and stagnant organizations and skills. Successful economies in the 21st century will be those that develop the best ways to foster organizational innovation and skill development, and we invite our readers to contribute to that agenda.

5. CONCLUSION:
THE DIGITAL FRONTIER

Technology is a gift of God. After the gift of life it is perhaps the greatest of God's gifts. It is the mother of civilizations, of arts and of sciences.
— Freeman Dyson, 1988

In this book we've concentrated on how our increasingly powerful digital technologies affect skills, jobs, and the demand for human labor. We've stressed that computers are rapidly encroaching into areas that used to be the domain of people only, like complex communication and advanced pattern recognition. And we've shown how this encroachment can cause companies to use more computers and fewer people in a growing set of tasks.

We see cause for concern with this phenomenon because we believe that one sign of a healthy economy is its ability to provide jobs for all the people who want to work. As we've shown, there's good reason to believe that ever-more powerful computers have for some time now been substituting for human skills and workers and slowing median incomes and job growth in the United States. As we head deeper into the second half of the chessboard—into the period where continuing exponential increases in computing power yield astonishing results—we expect that economic disruptions will only grow as well.

We've documented our concerns here and suggested policy changes and other interventions to address them. But we clearly are *not* pessimists about technology and its impacts. In fact, this was originally going to be a book about all the benefits modern digital technologies have brought to the world. We planned to call it *The Digital Frontier*, since the image that keeps occurring to us is one of a huge amount of new territory opening up because of technological improvement and innovation.

This image first occurred to us as we were conducting research to understand the impact of digital technology on competition in all U.S. industries. We found that the more technology an industry had, the more intense competition within it became. In particular, performance gaps got bigger. The difference in, say, profit margin between the top and bottom companies got a lot larger. This finding implies that some companies—the top performers—were racing ahead of the rest to explore and exploit new technology-enabled business models. They were homesteading on a digital frontier, opening up new territory that others would eventually settle in.

To build on this research we started collecting examples of digital pioneers and cutting-edge practices, and assembled a group of students and colleagues to brainstorm and do research with us. We called ourselves the "Digital Frontier team."

We changed course with this book because the more we looked, the more we became convinced of two things. First, that the issue of technology's impact on employment was a particularly important one. The Great Recession and the pace of technical progress have combined to make jobs a critical issue at this time, which is a difficult one for many people. When we think about someone trying to acquire valuable skills and enter or reenter the workforce now, we're reminded of the old Chinese curse, "May you live in interesting times."

Second, we saw that very few other people were focusing on the issues raised here. When discussing jobs and unemployment, there has been a great deal of attention paid to issues like weak demand, outsourcing, and labor mobility but relatively little attention given to technology's role. We felt that this was a serious omission and wanted to correct it. We wanted to show how far and fast technology has raced ahead recently, and highlight that current perspectives and policies will need to change to keep up with it.

But even after writing this book, we still firmly believe in the promise of the digital frontier. Technology has already opened up a huge amount of rich new territory and will keep doing so. Around the world, economies, societies, and people's lives have been improved by digital goods and high-tech products; these happy trends will continue, and likely accelerate.

So we want to conclude this book with a glimpse of the emerging digital frontier—a brief look at some of the benefits brought by the still-unfolding computer revolution. These benefits arise from the constant improvements summarized by Moore's Law and discussed above in Chapter 2, and also because of the characteristics of information itself.

A World of Benefits

Information doesn't get used up even when it's consumed. If Erik eats a meal, Andy can't eat it, too, but Erik can absolutely hand a book to Andy once he's finished, and the book itself (unless Erik has spilled coffee on it) is not in any way diminished for Andy. In fact, it's probably *more* valuable to him after Erik's done with it, because then they both have its contents in their heads and can use the information to collaboratively generate new ideas.

And once a book or other body of information is digitized, even more possibilities open up. It can be copied infinitely and perfectly, and distributed around the world instantly and at no additional cost. This is nothing like the economics of traditional goods and services that are the primary focus of standard textbooks. It can be a nightmare for some copyright holders, but it's great for most people. The two of us, for example, want as many people as possible to get a copy of this ebook as soon as possible after we're done writing it. Thanks to ebook platforms and the Internet, we can accomplish this vision. In the previous world of paper-only books, publication and distribution could take a year, and sales would be limited by the physical availability of copies of the book. The digital frontier has eliminated this limitation and collapsed timelines.

The economics of digital information, in short, are the economics not of scarcity but of abundance. This is a fundamental shift, and a fundamentally beneficial one. To take just one example, the Internet is now the largest repository of information that has ever existed in the history of humankind. It is also a fast, efficient, and cheap worldwide distribution network for all this information. Finally, it is open and accessible so that more and more people can join it, access all of its ideas, and contribute their own.

This is incalculably valuable, and grounds for great optimism, even if some things look bleak right now, for computers are machines that help with ideas, and economies run on ideas. As economist Paul Romer writes:

> Every generation has perceived the limits to growth that finite resources and undesirable side effects would pose if no new ... ideas were discovered. And every generation has underestimated the potential for finding new ... ideas. We consistently fail to grasp how many ideas remain to be discovered. ... Possibilities do not merely add up; they multiply.

It might seem as if we're short on big new ideas at present, but this is almost certainly an illusion. As David Leonhard notes, when Bill Clinton assembled the top minds of the nation to discuss the economy in 1992, no one mentioned the Internet.

Romer also makes the point that "perhaps the most important ideas of all are meta-ideas—ideas about how to support the production and transmission of other ideas." The digital frontier is just such a meta-idea—it generates more ideas and shares them better than anything else we've ever come up with. So either a huge amount of basic thinking about economics and growth is wrong, or a bumper crop of useful innovations will grow on this frontier. We're betting on the latter possibility.

At a less abstract and more personal level, the digital frontier is also improving our lives. If you have Internet access and a connected device today, it's both free and easy to keep in touch with the people who mean something to you—your kith and kin—even as you and they move around. You can use resources like Skype, Facebook, and Twitter to send messages, make voice and video calls, share still and moving pictures, and let everyone know what you're doing and how you're doing. As any lover or grandparent will tell you, these are not trivial capabilities; they're priceless ones.

Many of us use these resources so often now that we take them for granted, but they're all less than 10 years old. The digital frontier of 2001 was already wide, but it's gotten immeasurably bigger over the past decade, and enriched our lives as it has done so.

We see this same phenomenon everywhere we look. The developing world, for example, has been transformed by mobile telephones. We in rich countries long ago forgot what it's like to have to live in isolation—to have no easy way to communicate farther than our voices or bodies could travel. But such isolation was the sad reality for billions of people around the world, until mobile telephony came along.

Once it did, the results were breathtaking. A wonderful study by economist Robert Jensen found, for example, that as soon as mobile telephones became available in the fishing regions of Kerala, India, the price of sardines dropped and stabilized, yet fishermen's profits actually went up. This happened because fishermen for the first time had access to real-time price and demand information from the markets on land, which they used to make decisions that completely eliminated waste. Results like these help explain why there were more than 3.8 billion mobile phone subscriptions in the developing world by late 2010, and why *The Economist* magazine wrote that "their spread in poor countries is not just reshaping the industry—it is changing the world."

As digital technologies make markets and businesses more efficient, they benefit all of us as consumers. As they increase government transparency and accountability and give us new ways to assemble and make our voices heard, they benefit us as citizens. And as they put us in touch with ideas, knowledge, friends, and loved ones, they benefit us as human beings.

So as we observe the opening up of the digital frontier, we are hugely optimistic. History has witnessed three industrial revolutions, each associated with a general purpose technology. The first, powered by steam, changed the world so much that according to historian Ian Morris, it "made mockery of all that had gone before." It allowed huge and unprecedented increases in population, social development, and standards of living. The second, based on electricity, allowed these beneficial trends to continue and led to a sharp acceleration of productivity in the 20th century. In each case there were disruptions and crises, but in the end, the mass of humanity was immensely better off than before.

The third industrial revolution, which is unfolding now, is fuelled by computers and networks. Like both of the previous ones, it will take decades to fully play out. And like each of the first two, it will lead to sharp changes in the path of human development and history. The twists and disruptions will not always be easy to navigate. But we are confident that most of these changes will be beneficial ones, and that we and our world will prosper on the digital frontier.

ACKNOWLEDGMENTS

We've been talking about the ideas that went into this book for a while now, and with a lot of people. We found a fantastic group of colleagues in the Digital Frontier team we assembled—a group of students and researchers at MIT who volunteered a lot of their time over the course of a year to talk with us, hunt down facts, figures, and examples, and brainstorm about what was going on between technology and the economy. Team members included Whitney Braunstein, Claire Calméjane, Greg Gimpel, Tong Li, Liron Wand, George Westerman, and Lynn Wu. We're extremely grateful to them. In addition, Mona Masghati and Maya Bustan helped Andy a great deal with his research, and Heekyung Kim and Jonathan Sidi did the same for Erik.

We are grateful for conversations on technology and employment with our MIT colleagues, including Daron Acemoglu, David Autor, Frank Levy, Tod Loofbourrow, Thomas Malone, Stuart Madnick, Wanda Orlikowski, Michael Schrage, Peter Weill, and Irving Wladawsky-Berger. In addition, Rob Atkinson, Yannis Bakos, Susanto Basu, Menzie Chinn, Robert Gordon, Lorin Hitt, Rob Huckman, Michael Mandel, Dan Snow, Zeynep Ton and Marshall van Alstyne were very generous with their insights. We also benefited greatly from talking with people in industry who are making and using incredible technologies, including Rod Brooks, Paul Hofmann Ray Kurzweil, Ike Nassi, and Hal Varian.

We presented some of the ideas contained here to seminar audiences at MIT, Harvard Business School, Northwestern, NYU, UC/Irvine, USC's Annenberg School, SAP, McKinsey, and the Information Technology and Innovation Foundation. We also presented related work at conferences including WISE, ICIS, Techonomy, and the Aspen Ideas Festival. We received invaluable feedback at each of these sessions. The most important thing we learned was that the topic of technology's influence on employment immediately engages people's interest, so we shaped our research and writing accordingly. Techonomy organizer David Kirkpatrick has been especially keen to start a high-level conversation about computers, robots, and jobs.

We imposed on a small group of people to read early drafts of the manuscript. Martha Pavlakis, Anna Ivey, George Westerman, David McAfee, Nancy Haller, Carol Franco, and Jeff Kehoe all obliged and sharpened up our ideas and our prose. Andrea and Dana Meyer of Working Knowledge honed them both further while Jody Berman provided impeccable copyediting and proofreading. We are grateful to Greg Leutenberg for the cover design, and to Annie Hard, who converted our ebook into a professional-looking physical book using Amazon.com's CreateSpace utility.

The MIT Center for Digital Business (CDB) has been the ideal home from which to conduct this work, and we're particularly grateful to our colleague David Verrill, executive director of the CDB. David makes the place run beautifully; he'll be the last person ever replaced by a machine.

We claim sole ownership of virtually none of the ideas presented here, but we're emphatic that all the mistakes are 100% ours.

AUTHORS

Erik Brynjolfsson is a professor at the MIT Sloan School of Management, Director of the MIT Center for Digital Business, Chairman of the *Sloan Management Review*, a research associate at the National Bureau of Economic Research, and co-author of *Wired for Innovation: How IT Is Reshaping the Economy*. He graduated from Harvard University and MIT.

Andrew McAfee is a principal research scientist and associate director at the MIT Center for Digital Business at the Sloan School of Management. He is the author of *Enterprise 2.0: New Collaborative Tools for Your Organization's Toughest Challenges*. He graduated from MIT and Harvard University.

ENDNOTES

CHAPTER 1

PAGE

1   Aristotle. *Politics.* Trans. William Ellis. Middlesex, UK: Echo
      Library, 2006. Print

1   Economist Laura D'Andrea Tyson's calculations:
      http://economix.blogs.nytimes.com/2011/07/29/jobs-deficit-
      investment-deficit-fiscal-deficit/

2   Increase in unemployment between May 2007 and October
      2009: http://data.bls.gov/cgi-bin/surveymost?l

2   The mean length of time unemployed by mid-2011:
      http://data.bls.gov/timeseries/LNS11300000

2   Workforce participation rate:
      http://data.bls.gov/timeseries/LNS11300000

2   Proportion of working-age adults with jobs:
      http://www.usatoday.com/money/economy/employment/201
      1-04-13-more-americans-leave-labor-force.htm

2   Nobel Prize-winning economist Paul Krugman described
      unemployment as a "terrible scourge:
      http://www.nytimes.com/2011/05/30/opinion/30krugman.ht
      ml?_r=4&ref=opinion

2   Young graduates being denied the chance to get started on
      their careers:
      http://www.nytimes.com/2011/06/10/opinion/10krugman.ht
      ml?_r=2&partner=rssnyt&emc=rss

2   Don Peck described chronic unemployment:
      http://www.theatlantic.com/business/archive/2011/07/why-
      unemployment-matters/241658/

3   Megan McArdle asked readers to visualize people who'd been unemployed for a long time: http://www.theatlantic.com/business/archive/2011/07/why-unemployment-matters/241658/

3   Gallup poll identified "unemployment/jobs" as most important problem facing America: http://www.gallup.com/poll/148070/satisfaction-dips-june.aspx

3   GDP growth averaged 2.6% in the seven quarters after the recession's end: http://www.bea.gov/iTable/iTable.cfm?ReqID=9&step=1

3   U.S. corporate profits reached new records: http://blogs.hbr.org/fox/2010/11/the-real-story-behind-those-re.html

3   By 2010, investment in equipment and software returned to 95% of its historical peak: http://research.stlouisfed.org/fred2/series/NRIPDCA

3   The fastest recovery of equipment investment in a generation: http://www.epi.org/files/FigureA.png

3   The volume of layoffs quickly returned to pre-recession levels: http://www.theatlantic.com/business/archive/2011/07/why-unemployment-matters/241658/

4   Paul Krugman writes, "All the facts suggest that high unemployment in America is the result of inadequate demand—full stop.": http://www.nytimes.com/2010/09/27/opinion/27krugman.html

4   Peter Orszag writes "the fundamental impediment to getting jobless Americans back to work is weak growth.": http://www.bloomberg.com/news/2011-07-13/hard-slog-the-real-future-of-the-u-s-economy-peter-orszag.html

5   The average family in America earned less in 2009 than it did in 1999: http://www.theatlantic.com/magazine/archive/2011/09/can-the-middle-class-be-saved/8600/?single_page=true

5   Leo Tilman and Edmund Phelps agreed on stagnation:
http://hbr.org/2010/01/wanted-a-first-national-bank-of-
innovation/ar/1

6   Michael Spence has analyzed the great equalization in factor
prices like wages and its implications for convergence in living
standards: http://www.thenextconvergence.com/

6   Wassily Leontief stated in 1983 that "the role of humans as
the most important factor of production is bound to diminish
in the same way that the role of horses in agricultural
production was first diminished and then eliminated by the
introduction of tractors.":
http://books.google.com/books?id=p7w9lP2rZvcC&pg=PA77
&lpg=PA77&dq=The+role+of+humans+as+the+most+import
ant+factor+of+production#v=onepage&q=The%20role%20of
%20humans%20as%20the%20most%20important%20factor
%20of%20production&f=false

7   Brian Arthur argues that a "second economy" already exists in
the form of digital automation.:
http://www.mckinseyquarterly.com/The_second_economy_2
853

7   "The Rise in Long-Term Unemployment: Potential Causes and
Implications," does not contain the words *computer, hardware,
software,* or *technology* in its text.:
http://www.richmondfed.org/publications/research/annual_re
port/2010/pdf/article.pdf

7   Working paper published in 2011 by the International
Monetary Fund, titled "New Evidence on Cyclical and
Structural Sources of Unemployment":
http://www.imf.org/external/pubs/cat/longres.aspx?sk=24832.
0

7   Working paper published in 2011 by the International
Monetary Fund, titled "Has the Great Recession Raised U.S.
Structural Unemployment":
http://www.imf.org/external/pubs/ft/wp/2011/wp11105.pdf

7   Farhad Manjoo in the online magazine *Slate*, "Most
     economists aren't taking ... economy—so far remains on the
     fringes.":
     http://www.slate.com/articles/technology/robot_invasion/201
     1/09/will_robots_steal_your_job.single.html

CHAPTER 2

12   Arthur C. Clarke, 1962:
     http://www.isfdb.org/cgi-bin/pl.cgi?262388
12   Levy, Frank, and Richard J. Murnane. *The New Division of
     Labor: How Computers Are Changing the Next Job Market.*
     Princeton, NJ: Princeton University Press, 2004. Print.
12   Frank Levy: http://web.mit.edu/flevy/www/
12   Richard J. Murnane:
     http://www.gse.harvard.edu/directory/faculty/faculty-
     detail/?fc=321&flt=m&sub=all
13   The results of the first DARPA Grand Challenge:
     http://en.wikipedia.org/wiki/DARPA_Grand_Challenge
13   Google's announcement on its official blog:
     http://googleblog.blogspot.com/2010/10/what-were-driving-
     at.html
14   Lionbridge announced pilot corporate customers for
     GeoFluent: http://en-
     us.lionbridge.com/Company.aspx?pageid
     =2845&LangType=1033
16   Eric Brown interview: http://www.kurzweilai.net/how-
     watson-works-a-conversation-with-eric-brown-ibm-research-
     manager
17   Ken Jennings added "I for one welcome our new computer
     overlords.": http://www.aoltv.com/2011/02/16/ken-jennings-
     message-for-ibm-supercomputer-watson-jeopardy/
18   1965 article in *Electronics Magazine*:
     http://www.cs.utexas.edu/
     ~fussell/courses/cs352h/papers/moore.pdf

18   Later modifications changed the time required for the doubling to occur; the most widely accepted period at present is 18 months: http://news.cnet.com/2100-1001-984051.html

18   Moore's Law: http://en.wikipedia.org/wiki/Moore%27s_law

18   Martin Grötschel analyzed the speed with which a standard optimization problem could be solved by computers: http://www.whitehouse.gov/sites/default/files/microsites/ostp/pcast-nitrd-report-2010.pdf

18   Versions of the story the emperor: http://en.wikipedia.org/wiki/Wheat_and_chessboard_problem

20   Timothy Bresnahan and Manuel Trajtenberg note: Whole eras of technical progress and economic growth appear to be driven by GPTs: http://papers.ssrn.com/sol3/papers.cfm?abstract_id=282685

21   Economists Susanto Basu and John Fernald highlight how GPT allows departures from business as usual: http://www.frbsf.org/publications/economics/review/2008/er1-15.pdf

22   IBM's collaboration with Columbia University Medical Center and the University of Maryland School of Medicine: http://www-03.ibm.com/press/us/en/pressrelease/33726.wss

22   Nevada Department of Motor Vehicles regulations covering autonomous vehicles on state roads: http://alerts.nationalsafetycommission.com/2011/06/nevada-legislature-votes-on-driverless.html

23   Experienced doctors employ "intuition": http://blogs.hbr.org/hbr/mcafee/2010/01/the-future-of-decision-making.html

23   March 2011 story by John Markoff in the *New York Times*: http://www.nytimes.com/2011/03/05/science/05legal.html?pagewanted=1&_r=1&hp

23   Blackstone Discovery: http://blackstonediscovery.com/default.asp

24 Article in *Los Angeles Times* by Alena Semuels:
http://articles.latimes.com/2011/mar/04/business/
la-fi-robot-retail-20110304

24 During the Great Recession, nearly 1 in 12 people working in
sales in America lost their job:
http://www.theatlantic.com/magazine/archive/2011/09/can-
the-middle-class-be-saved/8600/?single_page=true

25 Humanoid robot falling down stairs:
http://www.youtube.com/watch?v=ASoCJTYgYB0

25 Quote attributed to a 1965 NASA report advocating manned
space flight: http://www.combobulate.com/techquotes.php

25 Kurzweil, Ray. *The Singularity Is Near: When Humans
Transcend Biology.* New York, NY: The Viking Press,
2005. Print.

26 Online generator of abstracts for computer science papers to
create a submission that was accepted for a technical
conference:
http://pdos.csail.mit.edu/scigen/
http://io9.com/5117892/computer+generated-paper-
accepted-for-prestigious-technical-conference

26 StatsMonkey:
http://www.npr.org/templates/story/story.php?storyId=1224
24166

27 The Loebner Prize:
http://www.loebner.net/Prizef/loebner-prize.html

CHAPTER 3

28 John Maynard Keynes, *Economic Possibilities for Our
Grandchildren*, 1930:
http://www.econ.yale.edu/smith/econ116a/keynes1.pdf

31 William Nordhaus: "to a first approximation, the economic value of increases in longevity over the twentieth century is about as large as the value of measured growth in non-health goods and services.":
http://www.nber.org/papers/w8818

34 The other four-fifths of the population saw a net *decrease* in wealth over nearly 30 years.:
http://w3.epi-data.org/temp2011/BriefingPaper324_FINAL%20(3).pdf

34 Franklin D. Roosevelt's second inaugural address in 1937:
http://avalon.law.yale.edu/20th_century/froos2.asp

35 Study by Steven J. Davis, Jason Faberman, and John Haltiwanger: http://econweb.umd.edu/~haltiwan/jep.20.3.pdf

36 Menzie Chinn: http://www.econbrowser.com/

36 Robert Gordon: http://faculty-web.at.northwestern.edu/economics/gordon/indexmsie.html

36 Paul Samuelson's research on outsourcing and offshoring:
http://www.ingentaconnect.com/content/aea/jep/2004/00000018/00000003/art00007

37 Clark, Gregory. *A Farewell to Alms: A Brief Economic History of the World*. Princeton, NJ: Princeton University Press, 2007. Print.

38 Efficiency wage literature:
http://isites.harvard.edu/fs/docs/icb.topic500592.files/yellen.pdf

39 Paper by Daron Acemoglu and David Autor:
http://econ-www.mit.edu/files/5571

40 Figure 3.5: http://econ-www.mit.edu/files/7006

41 Study by David Autor, Lawrence Katz, and Alan Krueger:
http://econ-www.mit.edu/files/563

41 Study by Frank Levy and Richard Murnane:
http://press.princeton.edu/titles/7704.html

41   About 25% of all agriculture labor threshed grain:
Clark, Gregory. *A Farewell to Alms: A Brief Economic History of the World*. Princeton, NJ: Princeton University Press, 2007. Print.

41   Jan Tinbergen: http://en.wikipedia.org/wiki/Jan_Tinbergen

41   Claudia Goldin and Larry Katz described the resulting SBTC as a "race between education and technology.":
Goldin, Claudia and Larry Katz. *The Race Between Education and Technology*. Cambridge, MA: Belknap Press, 2008. Print.

41   Studies by Erik Brynjolfsson, Timothy Bresnahan, Lorin Hitt, and Shinku Yang:
http://papers.ssrn.com/sol3/papers.cfm?abstract_id=166994
http://ebusiness.mit.edu/research/papers/138_Erik_Intangible_Assets.pdf

42   Foxconn currently has 10,000 robots, with 300,000 expected to be in place by next year:
http://news.xinhuanet.com/english2010/china/2011-07/30/c_131018764.htm

43   Frank, Robert and Philip Cook. *Winner-Take-All Society: Why the Few at the Top Get So Much More Than the Rest of Us*. Glencoe, IL: The Free Press, 1995. Print.

43   2008 *Harvard Business Review* article:
http://hbr.org/2008/07/investing-in-the-it-that-makes-a-competitive-difference/ar/1

44   CVS improvements propagated across 4,000 stores nationwide:
http://hbr.org/product/pharmacy-service-improvement-at-cvs-a/an/606015-PDF-ENG

44   Erik Brynjolfsson's research with Heekyung Kim on the ratio of CEO pay to average worker pay:
http://digital.mit.edu/erik/ITandOrg.html

44   Emmanuel Saez report:
http://elsa.berkeley.edu/~saez/saez-UStopincomes-2006prel.pdf

45 Kathleen Madigan's article about real spending on equipment and software:
http://blogs.wsj.com/economics/2011/09/28/its-man-vs-machine-and-man-is-losing/

46 Essay by Susan Fleck, John Glaser, and Shawn Sprague:
http://www.bls.gov/opub/mlr/2011/01/art3full.pdf

48 Discussion between Daron Acemoglu and Russ Roberts about the powerful and distortionary link between inequality and a non-level playing field:
http://www.econtalk.org/archives/2011/02/acemoglu_on_ine.html

48 Robert Reich's argument that a dynamic where superstars, given additional wealth, save most of it while their less-than-stellar competitors cut back consumption was in part responsible for the Great Depression:
http://www.washingtonsblog.com/2010/12/extreme-inequality-helped-cause-both-the-great-depression-and-the-current-economic-crisis.html

48 Arnold Kling describes on his blog a model where high-skill workers, given extra income, may choose to increase their leisure and savings rather than work extra hours. Meanwhile, low- skill workers lose their jobs, go on disability, or otherwise drop out of the labor force. Both groups work less than before, so overall output falls:
http://econlog.econlib.org/archives/2011/01/who_will_write.html

48 Joseph Stiglitz's article about the increasing concentration of wealth in a relatively small group:
http://www.vanityfair.com/society/features/2011/05/top-one-percent-201105

49 About 90% of Americans worked in agriculture in 1800; by 1900 it was 41%, and by 2000 it was just 2%:
http://www.ers.usda.gov/publications/eib3/eib3.htm

50 Research by David Autor and David Dorn:
http://econ-www.mit.edu/files/1474

50   Moravec's Paradox:
http://en.wikipedia.org/wiki/Moravec's_paradox

CHAPTER 4

53   Havelock Ellis, *Little Essays of Love and Virtue*, 1922:
http://www.gutenberg.org/files/15687/15687-h/15687-h.htm

55   Gary Kasparov writes about freestyle chess competition
between humans and computers:
http://www.nybooks.com/articles/archives/2010/feb/11/the-
chess-master-and-the-computer/

55   Technologists are making computers ever faster, smaller, more
energy efficient, and cheaper over time:
http://en.wikipedia.org/wiki/Moore's_law
http://www.economicsofinformation.com/2011/09/is-
koomeys-law-eclipsing-moores-law.html

57   The Long Tail of new products offered enormous consumer
value and is a rapidly growing segment of the economy.:
http://papers.ssrn.com/sol3/papers.cfm?abstract_id=953587

57   Abraham Maslow's hierarchy of needs extends beyond
material things.:
http://en.wikipedia.org/wiki/Maslow's_hierarchy_of_needs

58   Friedrich Hayek noted some of the most valuable knowledge
in an economy is dispersed among individuals:
http://www.indiapolicy.sabhlokcity.com/debate/Notes/hayek_
low.pdf

58   Technology enables more opportunities for what Google chief
economist Hal Varian calls "micromultinationals":
http://www.foreignpolicy.com/articles/2011/08/15/micromul
tinationals_will_run_the_world

59   The process of innovation often relies heavily on the
combining and recombining of previous innovations:
http://qje.oxfordjournals.org/content/113/2/331.abstract

62 Thomas Malone's article on the age of hyperspecialization:
http://hbr.org/2011/07/the-big-idea-the-age-of-
hyperspecialization/

62 Free online course on artificial intelligence:
https://www.ai-class.com/

62 MIT System Design and Management program:
http://sdm.mit.edu/

62 Khan Academy: http://www.khanacademy.org/

63 John Maeda's vision to move from STEM to STEAM:
http://www.forbes.com/2010/04/08/john-maeda-design-
technology-data-companies-10-keynote.html

64 2011 research report for Kauffman Foundation by E. J. Reddy
and Robert Litan:
http://www.kauffman.org/uploadedFiles/job_leaks_starting_s
maller_study.pdf

66 Skilled workers in America often create more value when
working with other skilled workers:
http://en.wikipedia.org/wiki/O-Ring_theory_of_economic_
development

67 Founders' visas in Canada: http://startupvisa.ca/blog?page=2

67 The American Society of Civil Engineers gives a grade of D to
our overall infrastructure at present:
http://www.infrastructurereportcard.org/

68 Banning layoffs paradoxically can lower employment:
http://www.nber.org/papers/w2056

68 Taxes on congestion and pollution can more than make up
for the reduced labor taxes: http://www.pigouclub.com/

69 Sonny Bono Copyright Term Extension Act:
http://en.wikipedia.org/wiki/Copyright_Term_Extension_Act

CHAPTER 5

71 Freeman Dyson, *Infinite in All Directions*, 1988:
http://www.goodreads.com/book/show/320561.Infinite_in_A
ll_Directions

72   We found the more technology an industry had performance gaps got bigger:
      http://hbr.org/2008/07/investing-in-the-it-that-makes-a-competitive-difference/

74   Paul Romer writes: "Every generation has perceived the limits to growth that finite resources and undesirable side effects would pose if no new ... ideas were discovered...":
      http://www.econlib.org/library/Enc/EconomicGrowth.html

74   David Leonhard notes that when Bill Clinton assembled the top minds of the nation to discuss the economy in 1992, no one mentioned the Internet:
      http://www.nytimes.com/2011/10/09/sunday-review/the-depression-if-only-things-were-that-good.html?pagewanted=all

75   Study by economist Robert Jensen:
      http://qje.oxfordjournals.org/content/122/3/879.short

76   *The Economist* magazine wrote that "their spread in poor countries is not just reshaping the industry—it is changing the world.": http://www.economist.com/node/14483896

76   The first GPT changed the world so much that according to historian Ian Morris, it "made mockery of all that had gone before.":
      Morris, Ian. *Why the West Rules – For Now: The Patterns of History, and What They Reveal About the Future.* New York, NY: Farrar, Straus & Giroux, 2010. Print.

79   The MIT Center for Digital Business (CDB):
      http://digital.mit.edu/

Made in the USA
Lexington, KY
28 November 2014